American Ferryboats

American Ferryboats

John Perry

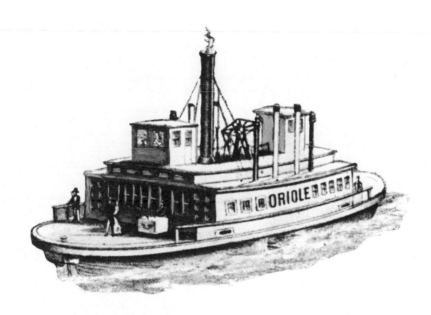

NEW YORK : : WILFRED FUNK, INC.

To Jane

CONTENTS

PREFACE

WHEN MY PUBLISHERS asked me to undertake the preparation of this book, I little realized that I was setting out upon what proved to be a wholly delightful adventure. The fact that I am a management consultant proved to be an unexpected asset, for in this profession I travel and I could visit many places with little added time or expense.

Most of these places were museums, libraries, and the collections of historical societies. Wherever I went, I found librarians and curators who were eager to help, who never seemed surprised at my ignorance, and who were so pleasant to talk with that I sometimes forgot my mission. I hope to write another book, if only to have an excuse to see them all again.

Several times I crossed the trail of Harry Cotterell, Jr., and, whenever I could, I went to spend an evening with him at his home at Newark, New Jersey. He, too, travels on business, and over the years he and his wife have built up— among other records—a huge card file. Each card gives the history of an American ferryboat: when and where it was built, by whom, and with what engines it was equipped; its name or names, and how it came by them; its specifications; its owners and routes; and its ultimate fate. Needless to say, Mr. Cotterell was helpful to me, both then and later, when he read the manuscript.

Before long I learned the rigid discipline a writer in this field must impose upon himself. Every source is fascinating. A single volume may have only a brief reference or two concerning ferries, but the temptation to sit and read became almost irresistible. Each source suggests another. One could spend days, or weeks, or years running down leads, chasing stray bits of information, seeking evidence that a ferry existed where logically there should have been one.

Since I am not, in the usual sense, a scholar and not a historian, I was able to stop far short of what could have been described as a complete history of American ferries. No other term seems quite right, either, unless it be "an appreciation." I've tried to write here the story as I found it, and to share with the reader some part of my pleasure in the quest.

JOHN PERRY

American Ferryboats

A Floating Section of Highway

CHAPTER ONE

A FERRY is a floating section of the highway. She shuttles between fixed landing points, across a river, a lake, or an arm of the sea. A trip on a ferry is but an incident in a journey by land.

The ferry is an unpretentious vessel. For her there is none of the majesty of a great ocean liner, nor the adventurousness of the wandering tramp steamer. She has no captain's table, no holds full of rare woods and fine whiskies. The ferry is squat and dingy, and she has often lacked even a name of her own.

But the ferry is the people's boat, and her history is theirs. Ferries carry more passengers than all other craft together, and for many of them a ferry trip is the only voyage they will ever make. An ocean cruise requires money, time, passports, reservations, packing, and endless complications. But the ferry is always waiting at the end of the street for anyone who drops a coin in the stile-box.

The ferry is humble, but she has carried presidents and kings, and ferries have played a not inconsiderable part in the building of America. Indian ferries carried Hernando de Soto and his men across southern rivers in 1540; Indian ferrymen carried settlers across western rivers three centuries later.

Ferries linked many of the colonial settlements. Dutch farmers of New Amsterdam commuted to their land in Brooklyn; Quakers living on the Delaware were ferried to their Meeting in New Castle; and Charles River ferrymen gave bargain rates when it was lecture day in Boston churches.

When America was new, rivers were the only inland highways. But these same rivers were often barriers to the overland traveler, save when there were ferries to set him across.

The rivers frequently were barriers to armies, too. Strategically they could be as potent a defense as a line of fortifications. General George Washington,

3

himself the owner of a ferry, well understood the importance of river crossings. With the ferry in his hands he could smash an unsuspecting foe camped complacently across the river. One winter's night in 1776 he did just that with a stunning surprise attack on the Hessians at Trenton, launched from the landing at McKonkey's Ferry in New Jersey.

The ferry could serve equally well in adversity. Washington's most daring retreat was the evacuation of Brooklyn in August, 1776. At night, after a battle gone awry, he stood on the ferry stairs while his entire command, its flanks dangerously exposed, embarked silently, covered by darkness and fog, under the very noses of the British sentries.

Ferries, like other civilians, have occasionally been summoned from humdrum lives to glory. Drafted into service, armored and armed, ferries became gunboats for the Union forces during the Civil War, and a few became flotilla flagships.

Rarely has the ferry been the star of a drama or comedy; but it has often been the stage. Seldom celebrated in song or story, the ferry has been the setting for a few great moments in history, for a thousand front-page news events, for countless narratives of people's lives and loves. Poet Edna St. Vincent Millay, for example, wrote the light-hearted *Recuerdo*:

"We were very tired, we were very merry—
We had gone back and forth all night on the ferry . . ."

Walt Whitman, too, loved ferries, because he loved people, and the deck of the Fulton ferries was, for him, a theater. Here is what he wrote in *Specimen Days* in 1882:

Living in Brooklyn or New York city from this time forward, my life, then, and still more the following years, was curiously identified with Fulton ferry, already becoming the greatest of its sort in the world for general importance, volume, variety, rapidity, and picturesqueness. Almost daily, later ('50 to '60,) I cross'd on the boats, often up in the pilot-houses where I could get a full sweep, absorbing shows, accompaniments, surroundings. What oceanic currents, eddies, underneath—the great tides of humanity also, with ever-shifting movements. Indeed, I have always had a passion for ferries; to me they afford inimitable, streaming, never-failing, living poems. The river and bay scenery, all about New York island, any time of a fine day—the hurrying, splashing sea-tides—the changing panorama of steamers, all sizes, often a string of big ones outward bound to distant ports—the myriads of white-sail'd schooners, sloops, skiffs, and the marvellously beautiful yachts—the majestic Sound boats as they rounded the Battery and came along towards 5, afternoon, eastward bound—the prospect off towards Staten island, or down the Narrows, or the other way up the Hudson—what refreshment of spirit such sights and experiences gave me years ago (and many a time since.) My old pilot friends, the Balsirs, Johnny Cole, Ira Smith, William White, and my young ferry friend, Tom Gere—how well I remember them all.

The island in the center of this drawing is Manhattan, as seen from Brooklyn sometime between 1836 and 1839. In between lies the East River. Beyond is the Hudson, or North, River, and beyond that, New Jersey. A ferry, probably the Fulton Street boat, is to the left of center. The three-decked sailing vessel on the right is a warship heading for the Narrows and the open sea. The tug alongside will cast off as soon as they leave the restricted channel. The artist, unfortunately, did not identify all those steamers with the remarkable lines.

Many of the old ferries are gone now. Morning commuters who once had a few breaths of salt harbor air on their way to work, sailing companionably down the channel beside a cruise ship tropic-bound, now must speed through holes dug beneath the river, or drive high above it, where the view is majestic but distant and brief.

One of the oldest ferry routes, the Indians' before it was Cornelis Dircksen's and Robert Fulton's, came under the shadow of the Brooklyn Bridge. Now long spans cross the Golden Gate, the Delaware, the Hudson, the Mississippi, the Missouri; and from the decks of ferries in the Straits of Mackinac tourists can see another giant bridge taking shape, which soon will bring an end to another old water crossing.

This is nothing new. In 1700 a bridge was built at Ipswich, Massachusetts, ending a ferry service begun half a century before. Another ferry was discontinued when the Charles River was bridged at Boston in 1786; the bridge was then said to be the world's longest. The Piscataqua was crossed by a bridge near Portsmouth, New Hampshire, in 1793. In 1808 the first major bridge was thrown across the Connecticut River.

Yet two hundred and fifty years of bridge-building have not brought to an end the story of American ferryboats. Several new diesel ferryboats are built each year. In 1955 the ferry *Del-Mar-Va* returned to the Little Creek-Kiptopeke run on Chesapeake Bay after a trip to a Baltimore shipyard, where she was lengthened by 90 feet; her running mate, the *Princess Anne*, was similarly lengthened in 1954.

Only a few years ago it seemed likely that White's Ferry across the Potomac, a short distance above Washington, would be discontinued. This crossing was known as Conrad's Ferry in October 1861, when Brigadier General Stone of the Union Army, in charge of the Corps of Observation, commanded troops on the Maryland side of the river. It was from Edwards' Ferry, three miles downstream, that the movement began which ended disastrously for the North at Balls Bluff on October 21, with Union troops trapped between the Bluff and nearby White's Ferry, unable to retreat across the river for lack of boats.

In 1953, White's Ferry was a pleasant place for a Sunday excursion, with picnic tables set out near the ferryman's house on the Maryland shore. The ferry, a scow powered by an outboard gasoline engine, had no regular schedule. It crossed whenever a car or truck sought passage; blowing a horn would summon it to the Virginia side.

The Coast Guard condemned the scow as unsafe in 1954—a view shared by more than one passenger. And that could well have been the end for a ferry off the beaten track.

But the ferry operators were optimistic, and in September they took delivery of a new 60-foot all-steel boat, the *General Jubal Early*, named for the Confederate leader who crossed here after a raid on Washington in August 1864. And in 1955 the ferry was busier than ever, with improved roads on both sides carrying heavier traffic to the landings.

The *General Jubal Early* is powered by an unusual means: a Hanley-Kermath hydro-jet engine, a gasoline-driven pump which draws in water and ejects it forcibly from an underwater nozzle. This is all the more noteworthy because it was on this same river, a few miles upstream at Shepherdstown, (West) Virginia, that inventor James Rumsey publicly demonstrated his steamboat on December 3, 1787, a demonstration he had been urged to make by his patron and former employer, George Washington. Rumsey's mechanical principle was unique. Instead of paddle wheels, his steam engine drove an underwater pump, which drew in water at the bow and ejected it forcibly from an underwater nozzle at the stern!

Thanks to the Coast Guard, White's Ferry now has a modern boat. But the American ferry has a timeless quality and the traveler who leaves the main roads to explore the countryside can still find, here and there, ferries which have changed but little over the years.

The double-ender *Eureka*, launched in 1890, is still operating in San Francisco Bay, the last beam-engined sidewheeler in service, according to the Steamship Historical Society of America. No teamboats—craft propelled by horses walking on treadmills—survive, so far as this author knows. But there are many current ferries still, flatboats driven only by the force of the stream. How many, and where they are, no one knows precisely, for these lesser ferries come and go today as in the past. In recent years I have come upon two current ferries on the Green River in Kentucky, one in Wisconsin, and one in Georgia. Another primitive Georgia ferry and one in Florida are illustrated in this book; the Georgia photograph was taken in 1941, the Florida picture a bit earlier.

LIBRARY OF CONGRESS

The exact location of this old ferry over the Oklawaha River in Florida was not given by the photographer, but it was probably Starke's Ferry, since replaced by a bridge. The picture suggests that this is a current ferry, but that is misleading; the raft is attached to a loop of cable run through pulleys on opposite banks of the narrow stream. An engine on the near shore drives the cable.

In the back country, ferry operations were and are so informal that keeping track of them would require a considerable intelligence service. A current ferry requires only a flatboat, a cable crossing the stream, and a few planks to make loading ramps—plus a ferryman. He will not venture across when the river is high or choked with ice, and summer drought may at times suspend service. If ferrying merely supplements his income, he may offer service at certain times or seasons only.

Such irregular performance would not be tolerated on a main route, to be sure, but the off-track ferry is a neighborhood convenience, not a facility for the general public. The ways of the ferrymen are known locally, and those who wish to cross the river drive to the nearest bridge when the ferry is temporarily idle.

In Kentucky, for example, interstate ferries and those along the main highways are regulated and supervised by the state government. But ferries along the secondary roads are sanctioned by county authorities, and a ferry is not considered abandoned until it has been out of service continuously for a year or so.

Even an earnest student of road maps may be unaware of the number of ferries still operating in America, unless his eyes are sharp. And even then he won't know about ferries too informal to be mapped. On most road maps, ferries are usually designated by the legend "*FY.*" in small black type printed over the blue of rivers, often difficult to see by reason of place names in larger type close by. A good map read through a magnifying glass will disclose many ferries, some unknown to people living hardly twenty miles distant.

Bridges cost more than ferries. The wider the river the more expensive the span, and the price rises geometrically. For a ferry, though, the width of the stream makes little difference in the cost. As little as a hundred cars a day may be enough traffic to support a ferry, while several thousand vehicles daily are required to justify a free or toll bridge across a river as broad as, say, the Ohio.

So, on the Ohio, there is only one bridge in the 145 rural miles between Louisville and Covington, Kentucky. The map on my desk shows no ferries between Louisville and that bridge, at Milton, 53 miles upstream. But only 15 miles beyond Milton is the ferry at Carrollton, which crosses to a point near Lamb on the Indiana side.

Eight miles to the east is a ferry from Ghent to Vevay; nine miles beyond that is a crossing from Warsaw to a point on Indiana route 156. From Warsaw to Rabbit Hash the map shows no riverside road on the Kentucky shore, but nine miles further on one comes to the Petersburg-Aurora ferry. Still another ferry is operating halfway between Petersburg and Covington, a straight-line distance of about 20 miles.

Once there were many ferries crossing the Ohio from Louisville to New Albany and Jeffersonville, Indiana, and several from Covington and Newport, Kentucky, to Cincinnati. But at these heavily-traveled crossings between neighboring big cities bridges did supersede the ferries.

This poses for residents living in that long stretch between Louisville and Covington a choice: to use the bridges, which might mean an extra hundred miles of travel, or to continue to patronize their local ferries. Naturally enough, many of them choose the ferries.

There is a third possibility, not so much a matter of choice as a change in the customs of people and the pattern of commerce. Ferries came into being for two principal reasons. Some, like the early ferries of Boston, New York and Philadelphia connected neighboring settlements within colonies. Others, like fur trader John Harris's ferry on the Susquehanna, were located at good crossing points to serve as links in an important overland route. These ferries attracted settlers, for there was usually good business to be done at junction points of land and water routes. Around Harris's ferry grew up a village, now the city of Harrisburg, capital of Pennsylvania.

LIBRARY OF CONGRESS

Harrisburg, Pennsylvania. The house is the home of fur trader John Harris, who operated a ferry at this point on the Susquehanna. Notice the Indians in the boat approaching the landing. More Indians are parleying with a white man, presumably Harris, under the big tree. On this side of the house a dog is in pursuit of what looks like a turkey.

But times change, and points once strategic may become backwaters. When most roads were poor and automobiles unknown, two towns linked by a ferry may have been nearest neighbors; but with modern highways their ties with other communities may be strengthened while those with each other wither away.

Some ferries are replaced by bridges. Some die for lack of use. Once it was ferries that attracted business. Now it is the bridges and highways that shape the flow of commerce, and the relocation of a main route can impose a virtual death sentence on a community.

So it was with Harper's Ferry, West Virginia, at the junction of the Shenandoah and Potomac Rivers. Robert Harper, native of Oxford, England, came here first in 1747, on his way to erect a meeting house for the Society of Friends at their flourishing settlement near what is now Winchester, Virginia. He was impressed by the possibilities of the rivers and the pass, bought land which was later confirmed to him by Lord Fairfax, and returned to settle. Around his ferry grew up a bustling, thriving town, a main crossing on the road westward through which thousands of settlers passed. It became a key point in military strategy. A bridge was built, and the railroad crossed the Potomac here.

But several low-level bridges were carried away by floods, and the steep, narrow streets of the town were ill-suited to a main highway. So, a few years ago, the route was changed, and U. S. 340 now by-passes Harper's Ferry.

Since then, the town has become partially a ghost city, with many vacant stores and buildings. Today it is slowly taking on a new life as a tourist attraction and resort. Its scenery was first made famous by Thomas Jefferson; the federal government has made part of it a national monument; there are many old buildings, including Harper's home, awaiting restoration.

Still fighting for life is the town of Toad Suck, Arkansas. According to local legend, Toad Suck, about fifty miles up the Arkansas River from Little Rock, took its name from that of a tavern frequented by thirsty boatmen who poled up the river years ago, where they sucked so much whisky they became fat as toads.

Surveyors' maps of 1820 show a ferry crossing here, and a ferry operated more or less continuously until World War II. Toad Suck, with a few hundred families, isn't on most road maps; it is at the point where State highway 60 meets the river, and an up-to-date map warns "No Crossing."

Conway, on the other side, is on the map, and this is where the people of Toad Suck went to shop, to meet friends, to marry, to attend church, and to bury their dead. Toad Suck is in Perry County, and many former residents of the county are buried in the old Red Hill Cemetery across the river.

Perry County has no Negro school; the children crossed on the ferry to a school at Conway. There are few physicians near Toad Suck. Today, for their shopping and medical care people must go to Little Rock, or to the nearer but smaller town of Morrilton.

When the ferry stopped, it disrupted a century-old pattern of living. Residents clamored for its return, but the State Highway Commission has hitherto refused, saying it would cost $46,000 a year to operate the ferry, and that there isn't enough traffic on Route 60 to justify it.

"Of course there's no traffic," one resident snorted. "Who but a jackass would use a road that runs right into the river?"

And so it does. The end of the road, no longer maintained, runs through a pasture to the river bank. Under an oak tree the hull of an old ferry lies on the levee, rusting away.

There are many Toad Sucks in rural America. On the other hand, many a ferry, once abandoned, has been put back in service, aided by growing population, higher incomes, and better secondary roads. In Arkansas the peak of ferry development was not in the 19th century but in the 1930's. The ferry is far from dead; indeed, even now, new routes are being studied.

In March 1955, for example, the Hudson River Day Line, Inc., entered into an agreement with the New Jersey Highway Authority providing for ferry service between Cape May, New Jersey, and Lewes, Delaware, a long crossing. The operators were to develop operating plans for speedy, convenient, safe and economical service to cross Delaware Bay from the southern terminus of the Garden State Parkway. As this book went to press the project was still under study.

Some day, perhaps, the ferries will be gone, but not yet, not for many years. Some ferries will be abandoned this year and some next year. But there will be some new ones, too, and perhaps the revival of a few once discontinued. Many ferries are gone, but some of the oldest still make their endless crossings.

PICTURESQUE AMERICA, WILLIAM CULLEN BRYANT, ED., 1872

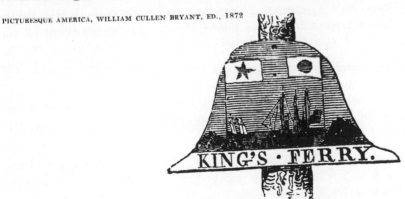

The signboard at King's Ferry, on the Hudson River.

t' Fort nieuw Amsterdam op de Manhatans

Early New Amsterdam. If authentic, this is the earliest (1626-1628) known view of Manhattan Island, shortly after its settlement by the Dutch. Ferrying was unorganized, those who wished to cross making the best bargain they could with Indian or white boatmen. See how differently constructed were the Indians' and the white men's boats. The Indian at the rear of the closest canoe seems to be the coxswain. It is difficult to tell whether he is instructing his own crewmates or calling to the Dutchmen in the other boat.

Redskin Ferrymen

~~~~~~

.

CHAPTER TWO

ON THE ISLAND the Dutch named Nieuw Amsterdam was a tract of land called by the Indians Sappohanican, about where Greenwich Village is today. Its western boundary was the North (Hudson) River, and on the east was a creek, Bestevaer Killetje, which emptied into the North River. Paddling up this creek, and through swamps and ponds, an Indian came to fresh-water Collect Pond, from which another creek, Old Kil, flowed into the East River.

Thus an Indian from New Jersey would cross the North River and pass by way of the farms at Sappohanican through Manhattan Island on an all-water route, thence across the East River to the landing at Brooklyn. The Dutch put their ferry landing at the same point when they began farming in Brooklyn; the Indian trail beyond it to Montauk Point became, in time, the Ferry Road.

As the Spanish explorers were the first to discover, American Indians lived in scattered settlements, some small, some large enough to give rise to the rumors which lured De Soto, Fray Marcos, Vaca, Coronado and the others on their desperately painful and costly quests. Almost all of these settlements were beside rivers.

Explorers generally followed Indian trails, and when they came to a stream too wide and deep to ford, there was likely to be a village, with boatmen able to take them over if an amicable agreement could be reached. In his expedition up the Savannah River and down the Alabama, early in his futile four-year search for treasure, Hernando de Soto found Indians using grapevine ferries, boats which they pulled across the streams by means of grapevine ropes stretched between the banks. One probable place where De Soto crossed the Alabama was near the present site of Claiborne, where a white man's ferry later operated for many years.

After the Spaniards had burned and tortured and massacred and pillaged their way across the land, the Indians knew what white men were: thieves and murderers when they smelled gold; formidable opponents in open battle; but at other times traders with whom one could strike a bargain. Wars were fought between white and red for more than three hundred years, but neither all the time nor everywhere. After the explorers but before the settlers came the adventurers and travelers, often in parties so small that they had no choice but to seek peace with the Indians they encountered.

Traveling overland, there were many rivers to cross, and the quickest way was to find an Indian with a boat. The Indians were quick to learn the ferrying trade and to appreciate the advantages of monopoly. Their distrust of white men helped make them shrewd. Finding that good bargains were seldom made at gunpoint, they were likely to negotiate from the opposite shore.

There is an old riddle about a man who had some fox and geese to ferry across a stream. He could not carry them all at once, but he dared not leave them together untended. Often the Indians constructed just such a situation to hold the advantage, offering only one or two boats for service and contriving to keep the white men separated from their goods as long as possible.

As the settlements of white men grew and the old trails between them were used more frequently, many Indians made ferrying a more or less regular occupation, breaking with their old tribal pattern of subsistence farming and hunting to live by the white man's money economy. About 1630 an Englishwoman, Alice Morse Earl, visiting the New England colonies was a passenger of one such ferryman and wrote in her diary how it felt to be carried in a birchbark canoe.

"The Canoo was very small and shallow, which greatly terrify'd me and caused me to be very circumspect, sitting with my hands fast on each side, my eyes steady, not daring so much as to lodge my tongue a hair's breadth more on one side of my mouth than t'other, nor so much as think on Lott's wife, for a very thought would have oversett our wherry."

The Indian paths became horse trails, and then the settlers' "traces." But the find-an-Indian way of crossing a river was typical of the frontier for more than two centuries. Travelers were still bargaining with red men west of the Mississippi in the middle nineteenth century, a couple of hundred years after regular chartered ferries were inaugurated in New England and Virginia.

The treaties negotiated with Indian nations often gave them exclusive rights of ferriage in their territories and, to a degree, imposed on them the obligation of providing ferry service. Difficulties often arose, as Acting Secretary of War George Graham complained in a letter to D. B. Mitchell, Creek Agent, on November 3, 1817: *

---

* *Territorial Papers*—The National Archives Record Service.

An Indian ferry. This wood engraving by A. Anderson shows an
imaginary but typical scene in colonial America. Two travelers following an Indian trail have come to a stream and arranged ferriage.
The view suggests that the scene is in one of the northern colonies.

"The citizens of Georgia and travellers complain much, not only of the road,
but of the impositions which they are subjected to by the Indians. As the Chiefs
of the Creek nation have refused to permit our citizens to establish public houses
and ferries on this road within their limits, I know of no way by which these complaints can be even partially removed, except you can obtain an article in the
treaty which you are authorized to hold, by which the nation will stipulate to keep
up public houses and ferries, subject to such *rates* and *tolls* as may be fixed upon
annually by the agent of the United States, and one or more Chiefs designated by
the Creek nation . . ."

Three months later, Mitchell reported success:

"At the late meeting the Chiefs have determined that the Ferries at the
Rivers on the Main Route from Fort Hawkins to the Alabama Shall be National
property. Hitherto they have been held by the Indians of Certain Towns, and were

a Subject of constant complaint as well as on account of extravagant rates being often demanded, as of negligence and inattention by which travellers were detained. The present arrangement promises to remove these causes of complaint as in the future they will be Subject to the immediate order of the Agent . . ."

It didn't quite work out that way, for Agent Mitchell, for better or worse, entangled himself in the ferry business and was shortly accused of reaping personal profits, a charge to which he heatedly replied:

"This Sir, is Scandalously false. The Ferry at Chatahochee is now in the possession of, and Kept by the same Indians who attended it before the Change; That at this place having been abandoned, I may say in the face of the whole Nation, for it was during the meeting in January last, by those who formerly kept it, I was under the necessity of taking one of my workmen from his employment and putting him to attend the Ferry at very high wages, since which two hands have been Constantly engaged in the same service . . ."

Mitchell appears to have cleared his name, but his efforts to improve the ferry service were less effective, for later in the year the Secretary of War sent him another bill of complaints, much the same as before.

William Bartram, naturalist and traveler, had a kinder word for the Indians when he passed through Alabama in 1776, crossing Pintala Creek on a grapevine ferry. He had a packhorse train load of goods to move, and the Indians kept his baggage dry by piling bundles of cane on top of the logs to form a higher platform.

Alabama has more large streams than any other state, which gave it the name of creek country and its natives that of "Creeks." Here there were many Indian ferries, the grapevine ferries found by De Soto and Bartram, rafts and dugouts poled through swampy water, boats paddled across broader and deeper streams.

Here, as almost everywhere, white men gradually took over the Indian trails as their own, and when there was enough profitable business to make it worthwhile, the white men usually took the ferries, too. One of these expropriated ferries is still operating today, across the Tallapoosa between Lineville and Wedowee.

The Indian trail leading to one of the crossings De Soto may have used became the Federal Road, now U. S. 84. In the early 19th century it was a main traffic point for settlers. When the Creeks made war in 1813 a fort was built here by General Claiborne, from whom the present city took its name. He kept the ferry in service, and it operated continuously until a bridge was built in the 1930's.

Further north were the Chickasaw ferries, one of them at Muscle Shoals. And the same pattern can be followed along many rivers, from Maine to Kansas to California.

The Winnebago tribe lived along the Rock River in Illinois, and they were ingenious as ferrymen. When a wagon came to their landing, they unloaded it and carried the goods across in canoes. The team was then unhitched and the wagon hauled to the edge, and brought around sideways to the shore, two wheels in the water. This side was lifted, and a canoe placed under the wheels, whereupon the opposite wheels were raised and the wagon floated out until they too could be supported by a canoe. The double boat was then paddled or poled across, horses and cattle made to swim, and all assembled again on the far shore.

This was at Dixon, where U. S. Alternate 30 and U. S. 54 now intersect, formerly known as Dixon's Ferry. It became an important crossing, a fact which the Winnebagoes exploited to the full, sometimes waiting to drive their bargain until they had ferried a man's goods to the far shore, leaving him and his wagon awaiting passage. As late as 1828 the only ferries here were Indian canoes. Jefferson Davis, then a lieutenant of infantry, crossed here once by building a bridge of ice blocks.

J. L. Bogardus of Peoria was the first to challenge the Indian monopoly, sending a man to Dixon in 1827 to build a shanty and hold the ferry. When he began to build a boat, the Indians promptly burned it and the shack, and sent Bogardus' man packing home with a warning not to try again.

The following year an enterprising French-Indian fur trader, Joe Ogee, married to a Pottawattomie woman, was more successful. He served as interpreter in negotiating the Treaty of Green Bay, in which the Winnebagoes agreed to permit a white man's ferry. Ogee then settled down and built that ferry. He was an active man with many interests, earning an exceptionally high income as trader for the American Fur Company. He sought legislation sanctioning the ferry, and also sought sanction from the Commissioner's Court of Jo Daviess County, but even before he obtained either he went ahead, and Ogee's Ferry flourished.

In 1829 the county granted him permission to operate both a ferry and a public house, and he sold a half interest in the ferry, perhaps to raise capital, but more probably to give him time to run his tavern. He brought a post office to the landing that same year, and the postmaster was his employee.

The court fixed prices for the ferry: 12½¢ for a man to cross; 25¢ for man and horse; 25¢ a head for cattle (but a yoke of oxen for 37½¢) ; $1 for a wagon; 6¢ per hundredweight of merchandise. The court fixed tavern prices, too: 37½¢ for each meal; 25¢ for feeding and sheltering a horse; 12½¢ for a bed or a half-pint of whisky.

Ogee repurchased the half-interest in the ferry in 1830 for $1,060, $360 more than his selling price, but his temporary partner had made improvements well worth the difference. In 1832, for an unknown price, he sold the ferry outright to John Dixon; so Ogee's Ferry became Dixon's Ferry and, in due course, the city of Dixon.

It might be noted in passing that in 1816 the Illinois Territorial Legislature approved a bill providing that all preachers be granted free ferriage anywhere in the territory. The following year, for unknown but probably entertaining reasons, this provision of the act was expressly repealed.

In the Year of Independence, the same year in which William Bartram journeyed through Alabama, the Spanish explorer Juan Bautista de Anza was returning from his second expedition to California and came to the Colorado River. His diarist, Fray Pedro Font, wrote * that they recruited Yuman Indians to help them, and Indians and Spaniards joined in building a log raft, choosing the Concepcion narrows for the crossing.

"Tuesday, May 14:—While the raft was being made, resort was had to the expedient of having the Indian women swim over with various things in their coritas and their large caretes (mud-and-willow baskets and trays), and they spent the whole day making their voyages in this way.

"The raft being finished, at noon a raft load, including some men, was taken over. They again took the raft apart and made two others, which were finished about six o'clock in the afternoon; and now the commander decided that we should cross the river. The rafts were loaded with baggage, and on one of them we embarked, the commander, Father Fray Thomas, I, and others, making thirteen in all. But as soon as we entered the river, the raft began to ship water . . . Two persons precipitately jumped ashore, and we eleven who remained on the raft were in no small peril; for aside from the fact that the raft could not be steered well because of its heavy load, and that it sank badly, just at the moment when it left the land a very strong whirlpool came and submerged it.

"The Indians now thought we ought to leap ashore, but Captain Pablo, who at the head was steering with great courage, thought otherwise. He considered the idea of going back as an insult, and according to what he said one would think he wished alone to carry us in his arms to the other side.

"Finally Pablo's view prevailed; they pushed the raft from the shore, and shoved us into the river, so submerged that I, although seated on top of a box, became wet to the calf of my leg; and it is to be noted that the raft must have been something more than a vara and a half high. Many of the Indians who were on shore and saw what was happening, immediately jumped into the water, and some forty of them, surrounding the raft, took us over to the other side in twelve minutes, with a great hullabaloo and noise, especially when we were in the middle of the river and a soldier fired his musket, a thing that they greatly liked . . ."

* Anza's California Expeditions

Many of the swimmers were women. The best of them all, wrote Font, was the daughter of Palma, Yuman chief. Their day's pay was a few beads.

Red ferrymen were first, and when passengers were few they often exploited their monopolies, sometimes shrewdly, occasionally with violence. But politically they were at a hopeless disadvantage, even when their chiefs successfully negotiated treaties confirming their monopolies in law. Once a ferry became really profitable, some white man soon managed to take over.

The usual method was to gather—or invent—complaints about poor service: that the Indians were lax, or that they charged more than the approved prices. When the official files held enough complaints, local officials felt free to push the Indians aside. The Indians had no lobbyists in Washington.

Sometimes it was done more crudely, by bribery or threats, or by sheer force. The military commander of a riverside post might ignore the treaty, authorize white civilians to operate a ferry from the fort, and see to it that they enjoyed a competitive advantage over nearby Indian ferries.

Whatever the method, the Indians were always the losers. By the time business was good enough to support a current ferry, a horse-propelled ferry, or a steamboat, the Indian ferrymen were gone.

When Is A Ferry?

CHAPTER THREE

ONE OF THE DIFFICULTIES in writing about early American ferryboats is that few records were ever kept, and of these, not many survive. Those which do exist are scattered, frequently as part of collections in which ferries and ferry crossings figure merely incidentally. Only a few ferries, such as the Fulton Ferry in New York, were considered important in and of themselves. Consequently, the possibilities of a formal history are remote, indeed.

While a few local historians have done a respectable job of writing the histories of a few ferries, they would be the first to acknowledge that their searches of the records were far from complete.

The collected Territorial Papers record hundreds of grants of ferry charters; but many of these charters were granted to persons who thought they might want to become ferrymen. Some never did, and other records report ferrymen who never received charters operating at locations unmentioned in the official papers.

For example, Cornelis Dircksen, which is only one of at least six ways in which his name has been spelled, is supposed to have been the first operator of a regular ferry service between Brooklyn and Manhattan Island. This is because there is a record of Dircksen selling his property and his right of ferriage to William Jansen on January 24, 1643. I can find no record of when or how Dircksen acquired this right.

Winthrop Sargent, secretary and often acting governor of the Territory of the United States Northwest of the River Ohio, signed more ferry licenses than any other official in American history. The last decade of the 18th century saw a tremendous boom in ferry business in the Northwest Territory, chiefly along the Ohio River. Even today there are at least thirty-four operating ferries crossing the Ohio.

Sargent, sitting at Cincinnati on February 18, 1792, granted to Robert Benham the right to operate ferries from his land opposite the mouth of the Licking River (which enters the Ohio between present-day Newport and Covington, Kentucky) "to both points of said rivulet on the opposite shore." In 1795 Joel Williams, and Gustavus Campbel and Ezra Williams, received licenses from Sargent for ferries from their houses on the Cincinnati shore to points unspecified across the river.

That same year Ezekiel Beasley obtained permission for a crossing at Cincinnati, and in June of 1796 Rebecca Cannada and Wert Miller were added to the roster of ferrymen. That September James Lawson was licensed to ferry between Cincinnati and Cabbin Creek, across the Ohio; Robert Adams was licensed in December; his route was to terminate on the upper side of Cabbin Creek. In May 1797 William Fee of Hamilton County received a license to cross to a point above Bull Skin Creek; in August it was Aaron Mercer. There were more than these, and, in addition, licenses were occasionally issued in blank.

An official record often tells only half of the story, because there are two sides to every river. Northwest Territory began at the Ohio, and its Governor had no jurisdiction over the southern shore.

HISTORICAL AND PHILOSOPHICAL SOCIETY OF OHIO

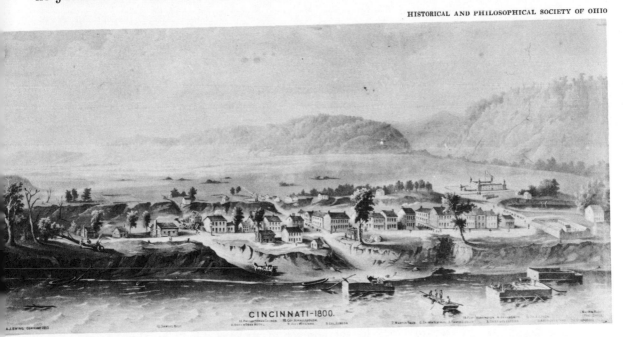

CINCINNATI-1800.

Cincinnati in 1800. The ferry is in the foreground, between the two river flatboats with steering sweeps. The house in the center foreground, to the right of the log cabin, is that of Joel Williams, ferryman.

Sargent's charters were not challenged, probably only because no vigorous authority across the river chose to dispute him. Wherever state or local governments faced each other from opposite shores, there was likely to be litigation. On the Delaware, Philadelphia and Camden councils both chartered ferries, and each challenged the right of the other to do so. Brooklyn and Manhattan had been embroiled for over a century at the time of the American Revolution. The heaviest legal barrages were hurled at each other by the state legislatures of New York and New Jersey, the latter at one time authorizing New Jersey ferrymen to seize boats owned by New York operators.

Philadelphia. This view of the Quaker City has been dated "prior to 1761" by the absence of structures built by then. At this time Philadelphia, with perhaps 40,000 inhabitants, was the second-biggest city in the British Empire. The flatboat (lower center, with the cattle on it) is typical of the ferries then in use. There seems to be an unequal division of work between the crewmen.

Much of the history of early ferries must be dug out of the records of municipal, county, and state courts. A New England ferryman sued to collect fares which a sheriff had refused to pay. This is the earliest known record that this ferry existed. A town council adopted a resolution calling on the local ferryman to give better service. Again, this is the first evidence that there was any service whatever.

Among the sources of information about early ferries are the journals of travelers who passed through America in early times. Combing through these journals is a fascinating task, much too interesting for a writer who must budget his time, for, despite the fun, his yield is scanty. Some travelers reported their journeys in minute detail, recording their impressions of birds and trees and animals, but somehow failed to mention the numerous ferries over which they must have passed. Some journals have been collected, edited, heavily annotated, and indexed, but the scholars who did all this considered ferries too unimportant to be worth an index entry.

So one must scan these records from cover to cover, and now and then the search is rewarded. But each find must be considered with some care and scepticism, for travelers often had only a vague idea of where they happened to be, and their spelling of names was often no more than roughly phonetic. Thus "Macby's Ferry" is the one elsewere called "McBee's and "Harspur Ferry" is Robert Harper's.

To make matters just a little more difficult, it was custom to name a ferry for its operator—and to change its name when a new operator took over. Thus Ogee's Ferry on the Rock River became Dixon's Ferry. An early Indian ferry in Alabama became Gray's, then Hatchett's, then Hughes'; and it could easily be confused with nearby Judkin's Ferry.

A secondary hazard of early official documents is the touch of the border attorney who, insecure in his legal foundations, sought to cover possible loopholes with successive layers of language. One such lawyer drafted the Bill of Assurances relative to the establishment of Little Rock, Arkansas, in 1821, and, with reference to ferriage, declared—in small part:

"... The Absolute exclusive right and privilege of keeping any publick ferry across the Arkansas river from any part of said Town embraced by the fractional section, and fractional quarter section aforesaid; Is hereby exclusively attached to Lot number One, In Block number one, and to the owners thereof, who ever the same may from time to Time happen to be—Which said Absolute exclusive right of keeping and public ferry from Said Town across said River, Shall forever be attached to, and go with the title of said lot number one, in block number one, a conveyance of which lot from one owner to another, shall be held and construed to convey as one of its rights and privileges, the said Exclusive right of keeping a public ferry from said Town . . ."

Somehow that sentence and/or paragraph managed to keep on in this fashion for an amazing distance, stating and restating the same Exclusive and Absolute right.

One could take almost any ferry, especially those which were established almost two hundred years earlier than Ogee's, and spend months piecing together the fragments of its history. And how many ferries have there been in America? No one knows, but the number of more or less formal, known routes has exceeded a thousand.

South Ferry at Shelter Island, New York, which lies between the two eastern arms of Long Island. This painting by H. Sandgam, though dated 1890, depicts a pre-1815 scene. Note the crude construction of the ferry, the use of both sail and sweep, and the off-center location of the rudder and tiller. It must have been an awkward affair to handle.

But, to be technical, when *is* a ferry? Only since the steam-powered double-ender has "ferry" suggested a boat of a certain recognizable shape. Canoes, rafts, dugouts, wherries, mackinaw boats, bull-boats, periaugers and pirogues, keelboats, cutters, sloops, skiffs, Durham ore boats, barges, teamboats, longboats,—these and other craft have been used as ferries. Anyone who lived beside a stream was likely to own some kind of small boat. If he agreed to carry an occasional traveler to the other side for a price, he might be considered a ferryman.

Place names are of some help to the researcher seeking the sites of old ferries: King's Ferry, Florida; Harper's Ferry, Iowa; Ferryville, Wisconsin; and Ferrysburg, Michigan; all these appear on modern maps. But Dixon's Ferry is now merely Dixon, Illinois; Harris' Ferry has become Harrisburg; and Wright's Ferry is Wrightsville. Burgeoning civic pride led hundreds of other towns to change their names.

Dobbs Ferry on the Hudson almost lost its name in 1870, when certain of its residents called a public meeting. A Dob family had settled there in 1698; the ferry was a strategic point in the Revolutionary War; Benedict Arnold planned to meet with Major André at about this point; and it was here that Sir Henry Clinton's representative met General Greene to negotiate unsuccessfully for André's life.

NEW YORK PUBLIC LIBRARY

This imaginary scene shows a flatboat ferry. Boats such as these were often used to cross shallow, sluggish streams. Note how the boatman poles his craft. Picture from a wood engraving by A. Anderson.

Delaware Water Gap, 1844. The second man in the ferry, just forward of the horse, seems to be poling the boat across from Pennsylvania to New Jersey. The Delaware here is normally shallow, though the current is rapid.

At the meeting, it was proposed that a new name be adopted, more in keeping with the town's elegance; the meeting's sponsors suggested "Paulding," the name of one of Andre's captors.

But an elderly gentleman arose and declared mildly that the real estate men didn't know their local history well enough. Paulding, he said, was not really such a fine fellow, and his part in the capture had been secondary. If anyone were to be so honored, he said, it should be the other captor, Van Wart. He thereupon moved that they adopt the name of Wart-on-the-Hudson. The meeting dispersed without action.

The most energetic conflicts among local historical societies arise over "firsts." Some claims have been put forward that such-and-such a ferry was the "first" in America. Even if one were so chauvinistic as to disqualify the Indians, a free-style "first" would be impossible to support. It would have to be heavily qualified: the first *legally-chartered* ferry offering *regular daily service* to the public *between established points.*

Local "firsts" are even more difficult to substantiate. For example, one highly-qualified historian, assisted by a staff of researchers, concluded that the first recorded ferry across the Delaware was at Christeen Kill, the first definite date October 1, 1669. But another student of local history refers to a record showing that a ferry was operating above Bristol beyond Penn's Manor as early as 1624.

But ferries are more than machinery, more than names and dates and places. They have been focal points for trade and mail and gossip, welcome breaks in the journeys of weary travelers, refuges for lovers, and adventure ships for children.

Progress: From Canoe to Horseboat

CHAPTER FOUR

THE DEVELOPMENT of the ferry is not altogether a matter of mechanical discovery and invention. The steamboat was a major technological step, but innovations prior to steam were, in America, primarily responsive to the needs of traffic.

If the first ferries were dugouts and canoes, it was not because people lacked knowledge and skill to build larger and better craft; they had, after all, crossed the ocean. But with no roads for wagons, there was little reason to build a wagon ferry. Nor, indeed, was anyone likely to give much time to ferrying as an occupation until the flow of travelers warranted.

The colonists came by boat, and they settled, almost always, at the water's edge. Settlements spread around bays, or upstream on rivers, and the people built small boats to cruise within their neighborhoods. A journey between colonies was most easily made by boat, especially if cargo were to be transported.

If a man wished to cross from one settlement to another on the opposite shore of a river or bay, and had no boat of his own, he could usually prevail upon someone to row or sail him over for a consideration. As settlements grew and spread, and there were more such passengers, men tried ferrying as a trade.

In 1630 the Court of Assistants of the Massachusetts Bay Colony invited persons to undertake ferrying service between Boston and Charlestown. A local resident agreed to do so, and a penny ferry service began, only to fail for lack of customers. In 1631 Edward Converse persuaded the Court to increase the fare to twopence, unless two or more passengers rode, in which case each was charged a penny. In 1631 another ferry was chartered, to Thomas Williams, who carried passengers from Winnisimmett, now Chelsea, to Boston for fourpence, to Charlestown for threepence. In 1635 Joseph Cooke established a penny ferry across the Charles from Cambridge to Boston; he offered half-price fares on Thursday, lecture day in Boston churches.

In 1637 the ferry business had done so well that the Court of Assistants decided to charge Converse £40 per annum for his charter. The following year he was enjoined to keep two boats, each manned by two men, on opposite shore, to provide more satisfactory service. By 1639 Converse had managed to have the fare raised to threepence.

These were ferries for passengers only: canoes or sailing wherries. A rider swam his horse across, holding the bridle, and there was no extra charge. According to some accounts, horses were transported on occasion; two boats were used, the horse's forefeet in one, hind feet in the other. The reader is free to believe this if he wishes.

A charter for a ferry across the Neponset River was granted in 1637, and in 1638 others were authorized at Weymouth and Scituate. In addition, there were boats providing service from Boston wharves to ships riding at anchor. Thus developed the complex of land-and-water transportation around the Massachusetts Colony, for traffic that was almost exclusively local.

While travel in these ferries was not quite as hazardous as the "canoo" crossing described by the nervous Englishwoman, it was often unsafe, and accidents were by no means rare. Cotton Mather wrote in his diary of a narrow escape: "A fearful hurricane and thunderstorm overtook us, just as we got out of Winnisimet Ferryboat (a ferry three miles wide), which, had it overtaken us four or five minutes earlier, we had unquestionably perished in ye waters."

A ferry from Salem to Beverly, operated by the town of Salem, was in business as early as 1636, charging town dwellers only half as much as strangers. It is also said that this ferry added a boat large enough to transport horses in 1639.

Was the 1630 ferry the first, as some claim? It may have been the first duly authorized and chartered by an official body, committing the ferryman to fixed rates and adequate performance, but there were certainly earlier ferries, even if one discounts the report of a Delaware ferry in 1624. The researchers of the Federal Writers Project in Massachusetts were reckless, indeed, when they referred to the Winnisimmett-Boston-Charlestown ferry as "the first ferry in New England and probably in North America."

New York seems to have no good entry in this contest. On the Brooklyn side, Dircksen's sale of his ferriage to William Jansen in 1643 is the first definite date, leaving to speculation how long he had been operating before he sold out. On the North River the first inter-colonial, or as we say today, interstate, route was the Communipaw Ferry granted to William Jensen by the village of Bergen, New Jersey, December 22, 1681. Much shortened in length, this heavily-traveled ferry is operated today by the Central Railroad of New Jersey.

The dates at which ferries were established are a rough index to the spread of population in America and the improvement of overland transportation. Thus in New England many ferries came into existence in the century following the early ones near Boston. Along the Connecticut River, for example, the Saybrooke-Lyme ferry began in 1662; Haddam-East Haddam, sometimes called Chapman's, in 1664; Hartford in 1681; Essex-North Lyme in 1724; Middletown-Portland in 1726; Knowles Landing in 1735; Cromwell-Portland in 1759; Rocky Hill-South Glastonbury at a less certain time, perhaps somewhat earlier than the Cromwell-Portland.

Bissel's Ferry at East Windsor is another claimed by some to have been the first public ferry in America, but it is difficult to read more than enthusiasm into their contention. It was not authorized until 1641 and was not actually in service until about 1648.

The Hadlyme-Chester Ferry. This is one of the oldest ferry crossings on the Connecticut River, and the ferry still operates. This undated photograph shows the steam ferry *Middlesex*. Notice how the funnel tilts to one side. There are a couple of big sweeps lashed to the cabin at left. The ventilator at the far end of the *Middlesex* suggests that this was a fairly deep-draft vessel.

Two of the old ferry routes are still in use along this river in Connecticut: the Rocky Hill-South Glastonbury, and the Chester-Hadlyme, established in 1769.

Also on the Connecticut River, a ferry was established at Springfield, Massachusetts, in 1674, by authorization of the County Court. The Court ruled that the ferryman could charge 2d. per foot passenger, and 8d. for a man with a horse. The tariff list included no vehicles.

It was many years before this ferry and others were linked together by passable roads, and before travel by stagecoach was common. Brissot de Warville, writing in his *Travels in America*, described such a journey by coach in 1788: "We passed in a ferry boat the river that washes the environs of Springfield." Then, later: "We passed the inconvenient ferry at Stratford." This was the ferry across the Housatonic near its mouth at Stratford, Connecticut. De Warville continued on to New York, thence by ferry to Paulus Hook in New Jersey where he boarded the stagecoach for Philadelphia, crossing the Delaware at Trenton.

Ferries large enough to carry horses were common in the latter part of the 17th century, as tariffs show. When Goodman Burrose opened his ferry across the Mystic River in 1664, he carried man and horse for a groat (fourpence), The Brandywine Ferry at New Castle, Delaware, charged 2 guilders for man and horse in 1675, 10 styvers for a man alone. Horseboats were then in use on many of the ferries near Boston and along the Connecticut.

Occasionally a wagon had to be carried, but it was usually disassembled and ferried across in pieces. Stagecoach service was not yet possible over most existing roads. The first overland mail service, carried by riders between Boston and New York, began in 1673. As late as 1760, indeed, there were only eight mails a year from Philadelphia south to the Potomac River, and the mail rider didn't leave until enough mail had accumulated to pay his fee.

The horseboat called attention to the problem of propulsion. Small passenger-carrying craft could be paddled, rowed, or, in shallow waters, poled. Larger ones had two men at the oars, or even four—two of them passengers drafted into service. But horseboats had to be larger, both longer and broader. They were far heavier, and rowing them against wind or tide was usually difficult and occasionally impossible. Consequently, sails came into use. On the Boston-Winnisimmett run a big sailing scow was put in service, large enough to carry twenty horses. The three-mile voyage often took an hour or two, as the clumsy vessel tacked up and down, trying to make some headway. On rivers such as the Connecticut, sails were of little use; the combination of wind and current could set a ferry ashore far below the desired landing-place, with little hope of beating upstream again in any reasonable period of time. To cross streams of that character, the rope or wire ferry was the first practical answer.

In the waters around Manhattan Island, ferrymen used several kinds of boats.

A pirogue. She has a blunt bow, a well deck forward, and a cabin aft for the passengers. The masts and spars do not suggest a very effective arrangement of sails. The flag indicates that this model was copied after a boat in use about the time of the Revolution.

The largest was the periauger, a barge-like sailing craft with high sides, with two masts, and often with a cabin at the stern for passengers. Under a favoring breeze, the periauger made a comfortable crossing, even in chill weather. But a shift of wind or tide could carry it far off-course, and a passenger for Brooklyn might be forced to land at Governor's Island.

Cattle were often ferried from Long Island, but the cattle boats were likely to capsize in a stiff breeze, drowning the animals and crew. Would-be passengers and shippers frequently waited several days for good weather before entrusting themselves or their goods to the ferries.

Several news accounts from the 18th century exemplify what the hazards of ferrying were in those days. On the afternoon of January 15, 1784 a ferry from New Jersey was trapped amidst floating ice. It was crushed, and sunk. All eight passengers were thrown into the freezing water. They managed to climb onto an ice floe which, as their wet clothes froze on their shivering bodies, was carried by an eddy around into the East River. Their plight was seen by persons on shore, but, as a newspaper reported: "All the slips being full of ice, it was with difficulty that two or three small boats were got out to attempt their relief; but the large fields of ice rendered every effort of the boatmen fruitless, and cut off every prospect of deliverance. Their position at this time was most perilous, involving the double danger of being frozen to death as well as washed off the ice and drowned."

As the floe moved up the East River, the tide turned, and it was carried down again to the bay, where rescue seemed remote. But one boat with a crew of soldiers boldly pursued the floe, found a passage through the ice field, and managed a last-minute rescue. Seven of the eight lived; one had frozen to death before help arrived.

In that year a Brooklyn ferry capsized when five horses became panicky and rushed to one side of the deck. A similar accident cost the lives of a ferryman and "five fat oxen." In April 1798 a periauger sank in a sudden squall; seven were drowned, one member of the crew surviving.

On yet another occasion a ferry set out from the Brooklyn landing in a light breeze; but squalls sped upon them and the passengers urged the boatmen to take in sail, which they refused to do. "Some of the passengers wished and talked of taking charge of the boat themselves," one of them wrote later. "We considered the boatmen incapable of conducting the boat, owing to intoxication."

But before the mutiny progressed from the talking stage, the first blast of wind struck, and capsized the boat. Of twelve aboard, only six were rescued.

There were other kinds of storms for ferrymen to cope with, not the least of which was amateur competition. While strangers coming to a river would usually patronize the ferry, local residents were seldom as cooperative, denying the right of any court to tell them how they should cross a river. Those who lived by the river and owned boats saw no reason why they should pay a ferryman, when they could row themselves over. Or, for that matter, why they should not transport friends and relatives, or, on occasion, contract to ferry a traveler for less than the ferryman's price. At times, while the ferryman was on the opposite shore, black market operators picked up passengers from his own wharf.

The governing authorities on Manhattan Island sought for more than a hundred years to control such bootlegging by Brooklyn residents, but never succeeded. Militant Brooklynites at times seemed close to a declaration of war on their neighbors across the river.

It began in 1654, with Manhattan and Brooklyn still under Dutch rule, when because of "daily confusion among the ferrymen on Manhattan Island, so that the inhabitants are waiting whole days before they can obtain a passage, and then not without danger, and at an exorbitant price," the director and Council adopted the first ferry ordinance. No one should ferry without a license, it provided; service must be regular and shelters provided on both shores; rates were fixed. But ferrymen would not be required to serve unless paid in advance, or "when the windmill on the battery of Manhattan hath taken in its sail."

Brooklyn had been colonized by Manhattanites, who went there first to farm, then to settle. The older Manhattan played the paternalistic role; the Brooklynites were rebels from the outset and didn't change when the British took over in 1664. Nor have they since. The ferrymen plagued the authorities to secure a monopoly; but the Brooklynites vigorously and sometimes violently asserted their right to ferry themselves, and to carry others at will. The river, they declared, was a public highway.

John Airensen, who leased the ferry in 1692, failed because of unrestricted competition. The New York Council promptly repeated its declaration that only the regular ferrymen should carry passengers, and put teeth in the ordinance: a 20-shilling fine for violators, one-half of the fine to be paid to the ferryman.

This had little effect, and when John Euwatse leased the ferry in 1698, the Council tried a new device: taxing food imported by ferry. But the Assembly knocked down this plan, and Euwatse asked to be released from his contract.

In 1708 strategy moved to a higher plane, the New York Corporation obtaining from the new Governor a revised city charter. Provisions of this charter gave New York not only title to the ferry, but also to all unappropriated land below the high water mark on the Long Island shore. Enraged residents of Brooklyn appealed to the colonial legislature and obtained a charter confirming their patent rights. But the next Governor, Montgomery, gave the New York Corporation an even stronger charter—so Brooklynites went right on bootlegging ferry trips.

King George II didn't confirm the Montgomery Charter, but in 1732 the colonial legislature did, in effect. But Brooklyn partisans went back to the legislature for rectification, and the contest see-sawed for several years. At the height of the row, incendiarists burned the Corporation ferry house in Brooklyn to the ground.

At last Brooklyn strategists succeeded in placing a case before the courts, compelling the New York Corporation to defend a suit against it for 5 shillings to test their right to ferry themselves. They won their case in 1775, but the Corporation appealed. But, because of what happened on July 4, 1776, the King's court never heard the appeal.

On that Independence Day, and, indeed, for another quarter century and more, the sailing periauger was the fastest and safest ferry in New York waters, if there were enough wind, but not too much. Elsewhere, in Alabama, Ohio, Illinois, California—almost everywhere except along the Atlantic coastal plain—the grape-vine ferries and dugouts and bullboats were the only ferries, there being no traffic demanding more.

All ferries of the time had one thing in common: service ceased at sundown. Occasionally a ferryman might carry a passenger after dark for double rates, but no charter required him to do so. There was little demand for service, for men seldom traveled the roads at night. They sought food and shelter, feed for their horses, a drink of whisky, and companionship.

Places of Warmth and Cheer

~~~~~~

CHAPTER FIVE

PEOPLE WERE SELDOM in a hurry in those days. Standard Time was unknown. The most reliable timepiece was the sundial, and each town had its own noon. The roads were hazardous enough by day; to travel them at night would be a desperate undertaking. So travelers kept an eye on the descending sun and made plans to be off the road before darkness fell.

The callings of ferryman and innkeeper were allied by the nature of things. Along the road, the ferry was frequently an outpost. If there were any settlement, it would grow up around the ferry; or the river settlement, if it came first, would require a ferry. The ferry was a natural place for the traveler to stop and rest himself and his horse, gather the local news, and plan the next leg of his journey. If, as often happened, service were halted by storm or ice or high water, the traveler would require food and shelter until he could proceed.

Passengers coming to the Philadelphia or New York or Boston ferries, even in good weather, might have to wait an hour or two for a boat. Many ferry grants required the ferryman to provide shelters at his landings, but he would have been likely to do so in any case, to fatten his income by selling food and drink to the waiting customers.

So the ferryhouse became an American institution, an often uproarious combination of tavern, hotel, restaurant, clubhouse, and market-place, with an adjacent stable for horses, and provision for extra overnight guests.

Most famous of all were the several built over the years at the ferry landing in Brooklyn. In 1655 carpenters Jan Cornelisen, Abram Jacobsen, and Jan Hendricksen contracted with the then ferryman, Egbert Van Borsum, to build one:

". . . thirty feet long and eighteen feet wide, with an outlet of four feet, to place in it seven girders, with three tronsome windows and one door in the front,

34

the boards to be planed and grooved, and the rear front to have boards overlapped in order to be tight, with door and windows therein; and a floor and garret grooved and planed beneath (on the under side); to saw the roof thereon, and moreover to set a window-frame with a glass light in the front side; to make a chimney mantel and the wainscot the fore-room below, and divide it in the center across with a door in the partition; to set a window-frame with two glass lights therein; further to wainscot the east side the whole length of the house, and in the recess two bedsteads, one in the front room and one in the inside room, with a pantry at the end of the bedstead; a winding staircase in the foreroom. Further we, the carpenters, are bound to deliver all the square timber—to wit, beams, posts, and frame timber, with the pillar for the winding staircase, spars, and worm, and girders, and foundation timbers required for the work; also the spikes and nails for the interior work; also rails for the wainscot are to be delivered by us.

"For which work Egbert Van Borsum is to pay five hundred and fifty guilders, one-third in beavers, one-third in good merchantable wampum; one-third in good silver coin, and free passage over the ferry so long as the work continues, and small beer to be drunk during work."

A "bedstead" meant bunks or berths behind doors which were closed during the day. The sum of 550 guilders is said to equal about $220, though my source is not clear as to how the rate of exchange was estimated.

Among those who visited the Brooklyn ferry house a few years later was one Henry C. Murphy, who wrote this in his Journal about tavern life: "It was the business of the good vrow, or her maid, to show up the traveller, and open the doors in the smooth partition of the box which was to receive his weary limbs for the night, and which otherwise he might not be able to discover, and after he crept into it, to come back again and blow out the candle, and in the morning to draw the curtains of the window at the hour he fixed to rise. There was generally one room in which all the guests were received, and where there was a pleasant reunion in the evening, and all the visitors ate, drank, and smoked. It had in one corner a closet which, when opened (and, honestly, it was not unfrequently opened), disclosed sundry decanters, glasses, and black bottles; and, on one side of the room, a rack in which were suspended, by their bowls, a score or two of very long pipes, each one inscribed with the name of a neighbor, its owner . . ."

Van Borsum did well as a tavern operator, though he sometimes had difficulty collecting his bills. Once he had to sue the Attorney General, Cornelis Van Tienhoven, for liquors and ferriage. On another occasion he confronted the court with a difficult decision: he had served a banquet to fourteen men, none of whom denied that the debt was owing, but each disclaimed responsibility for the party. This must have been quite a party, for the bill came to more than nine dollars per man; if the Brooklyn historian computed the exchange correctly, the bill was more than half the original cost of the ferryhouse itself! There is no record that he collected.

The "good vrow" was Van Borsum's wife, Annetje. Van Borsum died, but she continued to run the tavern until the British took Brooklyn from the Dutch in 1664.

A larger ferry house was built in 1700, a brick building, 24 by 40 feet, two stories, with five chimneys, at a cost of £435, ferryman John Euwatse being the first operator. This house was gutted by fire in 1748. It was replaced by a still larger stone building, known as Corporation House or Ferry Tavern, except for one period of its history, when it became Looseley and Elms' King's Head Tavern.

Just before the Battle of Brooklyn in the Revolutionary War, the ferrymaster and tavern-keeper was Adolph Waldron. An ardent revolutionist, he raised a com-

Brooklyn in 1746. This is the Brooklyn Ferry, at the foot of what became Fulton Street. Both rowboats and sailing flatboats were used as ferries. The penned cattle at the left are waiting for transportation to Manhattan, just across the river. The tall building at the right is the ferry house. It seems not to be the house discussed in the text. The Brooklyn Bridge now crosses the East River at about this point.

THE MARINERS' MUSEUM, NEWPORT NEWS, VIRGINIA

pany of light-horse and went off to the wars as its commander. But the British chased General Washington's army off Long Island and during the occupation the authorities gave the tavern to Messrs. Looseley and Elms, a pair of loyalist residents, and it became the favorite off-duty hangout for British officers.

The winter of 1780-81 was one of the coldest on record. The East River froze to midstream, and Long Island farmers had to drive their wagons far out on the ice before their produce could be transferred to boats. American Revolutionary forces moved troops and cannon over the ice from New Jersey to Staten Island. But in the King's Head Tavern a huge fire was always blazing. British officers warmed their backsides before it while Looseley and Elms busied themselves with decanters and carving-knives.

The season ran on, spring came, and in June they posted great bills:

This day being Wednesday, the 20th of June, will be exhibited at Brooklyn Ferry, A BULL-BAITING after the true English manner. Taurus will be brought to the ring at half-past three o'clock; some good dogs are already provided, but every assistance of that sort will be esteemed a favor. A dinner exactly British will be upon Looseley's table at eleven o'clock, after which there is no doubt but that the song of 'Oh! the Roast Beef of Old England!' will be sung with harmony and glee.

On other occasions there was fox-hunting, and "Breakfasting and Relishes until the Races commence." In 1781 Looseley advertised a lottery, with a grand prize of $12,500. Thanks to the tavern, "liberated" by the King's army, the two gentlemen had clearly become very rich. How much of their good fortune they retained when their British protectors were defeated is unknown. They lost the ferry, and municipal authorities resumed the chartering power.

Roast beef was not the only attraction of the ferry tavern. There was also the Gowanus oyster. A post-Revolutionary Brooklyn ferryman, William Furman, lived in a large house with a long, high piazza just in front of the ferry stairs. In the basement was his oyster house, where one could eat his fill of roasted oysters for half a shilling. A visitor wrote:

"We found a good fire, half-way up the chimney, of clear oak and hickory, of which they made not the least scruple of burning profusely . . . There had been already thrown upon it, to be roasted, a pail full of Gowanes oysters, which are the best in the country. They are fully as good as those of England, and better than those we eat at Falmouth. I had to try some of them raw. They are large and full, some of them not less than a foot long, and they grow sometimes ten, twelve, and sixteen together, and are then like a piece of rock. Others are young and small. In consequence of the great quantities of them, everybody keeps the shells for the purpose of burning them into lime. They pickle the oysters in small casks, and send them to Barbadoes and the other islands. We had for supper a roasted haunch of venison, which he had bought of the Indians for three guilders . . . We were also served with wild turkey and wild goose. Every thing we had was the natural production of the country."

A certain amount of overland traffic moved between New York and Philadelphia before stagecoach days. From New York there were several ways to start the journey. Beginning in 1661, William Jansen offered ferry service across the North River to Bergen three times a week by rowboat, or, if a horse were to be carried, in a flat-bottomed sloop. In the very early Eighteenth Century travelers from Manhattan could ferry to Brooklyn, and then "keeping the marked trees on their right side," proceed down to Yellow Hook (Bay Ridge) and across the Narrows to Sand Bay, Staten Island. After crossing the island to Smoking Point (now Rossville), they could take the Blazing Star Ferry over the Achter Kil to Sewaren, New Jersey. From there the route led to the Raritan River, where John Inian had established a ferry in 1686 on the present site of New Brunswick.

The first Delaware crossing at Philadelphia was offered about 1681 by Richard Arnold and William Cooper. The latter was the first of a family of ferrymen to operate from Cooper's Point at Camden, New Jersey. And, as mentioned in Chapter Three, there was a crossing at Christeen Kill in 1669, and perhaps, a much earlier ferry, above Penn's Manor, in 1624.

Other ferries and other routes opened in the next few decades. One of the early road promoters was John Reading, who proposed a better way to Philadelphia by crossing the Delaware at his landing at Stockton, New Jersey, some miles above Trenton. The Old York Road, Reading's venture, began on the opposite shore and ran south to Philadelphia.

In 1718 John Wells obtained a license from the General Assembly of Pennsylvania to establish a ferry "for the ready accommodation of persons traveling from this province to the Jersies and New York." Wells' ferry was a few miles below Reading's, crossing between New Hope, Pennsylvania and Lambertville, New Jersey. Both towns have Ferry Streets today (one block below their Bridge Streets). Two other New York-to-Philadelphia routes were operating by 1730. One began at South Amboy, New Jersey, across from Staten Island, overland to Burlington, New Jersey, where travelers boarded sloops to complete the journey. A parallel route began at Inian's Ferry in New Brunswick, overland to Trenton, thence by sloop. Post boys were carrying the mail weekly by 1739.

With heavier travel, it became worthwhile to improve the roads, at least enough for a farm wagon. From the Conestoga Valley in Lancaster County, Pennsylvania, came a six-horse wagon admirably suited to the rocky, sandy, muddy trails and the numerous fords. It was built to be strong but light, reinforced with ironwork from the smithy at the joints, and braced with riveted strap-iron. The Conestoga was boat-shaped, its bottom curving up fore and aft, and to the sides; in the spring freshets it might have to serve as a boat, being floated across streams too deep to ford.

The sides were high and box-like, the top of white homespun lashed over wooden bows. Fixed to one side was a tool-box, often ornately decorated, and the wagoner had to be as much an ingenious mechanic as a bold driver.

Conestoga wagons were often painted in bright colors; but the best workmanship went into the wheels, for they had to withstand the worst kind of punishment. Six sections of strong, seasoned wood were carefully pieced together for the rim. Twelve spokes were hand-hewn for each wheel and nicely fitted into hub and rim. A broad, heavy iron tire was shrunk on. A stout pin locked the wheel on its axle, and the wagoner carried a supply of tallow for lubricant.

These wagons were for freight. The driver rode a saddle horse, so that he could study the condition of a ford or a muddy stretch before committing his vehicle.

The roads reached out slowly from the cities to nearby towns, and by the early 1750's passengers could ride in wagons or coaches at least part of the way from New York to Philadelphia. In 1752 Joseph Borden advertised that he could transport passengers between the two colonial cities in 30 to 40 hours, but this was driving time; with allowance for stopovers and delays, three full days was considered good speed. The coach of the Royal Mail was operating by about 1756. In 1764 a new company improved service by taking passengers across the ferry at Trenton, then by road into Philadelphia. At about the same time the dangerous ferry trip from South Amboy to Staten Island was made unnecessary by improvement of the post road from Inian's Ferry to Elizabeth Town, where a ferry to Staten Island had been operating since 1669, and is still operating today. At Elizabeth Town one could board a sailing ferry for the long voyage to New York, also. But it was safer to make the short crossing to Staten Island, travel a short way by land, ferry to Bergen Point (Jersey City), go by post road to Paulus Hook, then ferry to Manhattan.

In 1771 Joseph Mercereau's "Flying Machine" cut the travel time between the two cities to, with luck, two days. Thereafter roads were improved and coaches became heavier and safer; but two days was the best time offered until the railroads came through.

Despite other routes to New York, the heaviest ferry traffic on the Delaware was always at Philadelphia, for there were Quaker colonies on both sides of the river, and farm produce for the city came in through Gloucester County in New Jersey. William Cooper is said to have opened the ferry between Philadelphia and Cooper's Point in 1681; others say 1688. In any event, by the latter year his boats were large enough to carry 12 passengers, two men at the oars, a helmsman, and a bowman. The bowman was, perhaps, superfluous in calm summer weather, but in winter there were never too many hands, especially when boats had to be hauled part-way over the ice, on runners fitted to the bottom for this purpose.

Authorities do not agree on the number of ferries established between Philadelphia and Camden, nor on the succession of ferrymen. William Cooper's original colleague in 1681, Richard Arnold, drops from the story almost at once. A license was granted to Daniel Cooper in 1695, but in 1708 William Cooper conveyed to his son Joseph a tract of land on the Jersey side and his ferry rights. The County Court of Gloucester gave a franchise to William Roydon in 1688, thus touching off a long legal battle between New Jersey and Pennsylvania jurisdictions. Roydon was permitted to charge sixpence for passenger, twelve for man and horse, and sixpence each for swine, cattle, and sheep.

Joseph Cooper passed on the ferry rights to his son, Benjamin, in 1728, who operated the ferry until 1769. Then it came into the possession of Samuel Cooper, who built a large ferryhouse later known as the Cooper's Point Hotel. Another William Cooper came along in 1800, and he became the first of the line to operate a steam-powered ferry.

An advertisement published in 1761 suggests what facilities a ferryman was expected to offer his clientele:

> As the Mayor and the Corporation of the City of Philadelphia have been pleased to grant me the Privilege of a Ferry, now carried on from the lower end of Arch-Street, at the sign of The Boy and Boat, to the two Ferries of Messieurs COOPER's in New-Jersey, directly opposite to this, I beg leave to inform the Public, that I have built a large, commodious House for the Entertainment of all Travellers, with Out-houses and Stores; also a Number of well-built Boats, calculated and fitted for a Ferry. And I have also added to my old Wharff a new Slip, which extends between 40 and 50 Feet out into the Delaware, to Low-water Mark, and have fixed a Pair of Steps to the Side of my Wharff, which makes Landing any Time of Tide, safe and pleasant for Passengers, easy for Carriages, Horses, Hogsheads, Barrels, or any Merchandize. The Out-houses and Stores are particularly intended for the Use and Security of the Goods of Market People. Dispatch, Industry and great Care, with due Attendance, will be given by SAMUEL AUSTIN at the NEW FERRY-HOUSE.

As roads improved and travel increased, as travelers moved westward, ferries and ferry-houses grew and thrived. The ferryman who once fed and bedded occasional travelers in his own home found himself the proprietor of an inn, and hired others to tend the ferry for him.

Susanna and John Wright settled by the Susquehanna in 1730, and Wright's Ferry across the mile-wide stream became an important crossing. Mrs. Anne Royall was a passenger once and wrote: "The sight of the river was terrific, the waves rolling high, the ice running, and a demi-flood from the melting of the snow, and nothing but a skiff to cross on."

The weekly post and express was running between Philadelphia and Bethlehem in 1742, and a ferry across the Lehigh River operated until 1800 or later; this was an unusual flatboat, being drawn across the river by teams of horses on land.

Westward the settlers moved, clustering around Harris' and Harper's Ferry, and moving on to build settlements on the Ohio at Pittsburgh and Wheeling, and then to the Northwest Territory. Before the end of the 18th century the Conestoga wagons were forcing their way across the mountains to Pittsburgh, linking the waters of the East and the West. Turnpikes were built by private companies, with tollgates to tax those who used them. The federal government entered the road-building business in 1818, constructing the first national road from Cumberland, Maryland, on the Potomac River, to Wheeling on the Ohio.

To encourage entrepreneurs to build roads and ferries, national and state governments often made grants of land, as was done later to stimulate railroad construction. One such grant was made to Ebenezer Zane, who opened Zane's Ferry on the Muskingum, where Zanesville is today.

As traffic increased, ferry monopolies became exceedingly profitable. Even before the Gold Rush, when the lines of waiting travelers were at times eight to ten miles long, people had often to wait several days for their turn at the crossing. All the while the ferryhouse did a rushing business. The owners of the Ingles Ferry across New River on the Wilderness Road to Kentucky were said to have earned $15,000 a year from their ferry alone.

Often the ferry itself was, to the ferryman, a necessary nuisance. For ferrying a passenger he might receive a quarter dollar, and earn his money by hard and sometimes dangerous work. By providing him with a bed, feeding him dinner and breakfast, selling him whisky, and caring for his horse, he would collect as much as a dollar and a half.

Joe Ogee opened his ferry on the Rock River, then a tavern, and before long sold his ferry rights to another man, finding the tavern more lucrative. Mark Beaubien, Chicago's first licensed ferryman, built the Old Sauganash, an inn that became famous as a house of entertainment; Beaubien was at best an indifferent ferryman.

A few of the old ferry houses still stand, though most are long gone. One, now a state monument, is the tavern which was built on the New Jersey side of McKonkey's Ferry on the Delaware, just above Trenton.

McKonkey's Ferry was one of those brought under military control early in the Revolution. In August, 1776, the State Convention at New Brunswick, New Jersey, ordered "That to prevent Desertion, no person or persons belonging to, or coming from, the army of the State of New-Jersey, be permitted to go over any of the ferries in, or travel through said State, without a pass signed either by General Mercer, General Dickinson, General Livingston, Colonel Griffin, or Colonel Biddle."

But that winter McKonkey's Ferry was no longer under American control. The Continental Army was shaken by its disasters at Long Island and Fort Washington, and American troops had taken refuge in the hills of Bucks County, Pennsylvania. It was the British who controlled the New Jersey side now, though they could hardly be said to control the river, since the retreating Americans had managed to lay hands on most of the available boats and secure them on the opposite shore.

Many of these boats were of a special type, designed about 1750 by Robert Durham for use at the Durham iron furnace near Easton. The Durham ore boats were of shallow draft, and flat-bottomed with sharp bows. They were over sixty feet long and eight feet wide, and were capable of carrying up to 15 tons of cargo. Propelled by poles, oars, or sail, they had become the principal working boat all along the Delaware and its tributaries.

Thus caught between the two armies, McKonkey's Ferry was practically shut down that December. But it was just as well, for the winter was cold and the river choked with ice. Customers were plentiful at the tavern, however, though most of them wore red coats.

Late on Christmas Day the rush of business was over. Most of the local regulars had celebrated at home that day, and the Hessian celebrators had made their way back to their quarters in Trenton.

The fire was dying to embers when the door opened and a tall stranger entered. More logs were quickly thrown on so Lieutenant General George Washington could warm himself after his chilly trip across the river in a Durham ore boat. He stood there for a time before the fire, talking with his aides, while his troops were ferried across to McKonkey's landing. Then they all set forth quietly down the road to Trenton . . .

The Current Ferries

~~~~~~

CHAPTER SIX

ONE OF THE journal-writing English travelers who wandered through America in our pioneer days was Fortescue Cumings. He crossed the Susquehanna at Harris' Ferry on his way to the Ohio, describing the ferry as "a large flat, with the western mail and several passengers and horses." It was winter; the ferry became jammed in the ice, and it took all the efforts of ferryman, passengers, and hands from shore to force it through.

After crossing the Ohio, Cumings proceeded to Marietta, on the Muskingum, and here he found a ferry which captured his interest, for it seemed to him marvelously ingenious. "The Muskingum," he wrote, "is about two hundred yards wide, and has a rapid current of from three to four miles an hour, by which the ferryboat is carried across in something more than a minute, by a very simple but ingenious piece of machinery. A rope of five or six inches in circumference is extended across from bank to bank, and hove taut by a windlass: two rollers play on it fixed in a box to each end of which the ends of two smaller ropes are fastened, whose other ends are led to the two extremities of the ferry flat, and taken round winches with iron cranks . . . on which the rope at the end of the flat which is to be foremost being wound up, presents the side of the flat to the current at an angle of about thirty degrees. It is then pushed off—the current acts upon it, and it arrives at the opposite side in the time above-mentioned."

What Cumings had seen was a current ferry. Given a flowing stream, one needs some arrangement of cables to hold the ferry against the force of the current, as the string of a kite holds it against the wind. If, then, a flat surface, either the side of the boat or a centerboard, is placed at an angle to the current's force, it will be deflected, and pushed to one side.

44

The accompanying photograph illustrates how this is done. To cross the stream, the bow line is shortened, pulling the nose closer to the cable, and the stern line lengthened. To return, this procedure is reversed.

F. G. de Fontaine described a current ferry on the French Broad River in Tennessee which he visited about 1870; but the artist, Harry Fenn, who drew a picture of it somehow missed the point. Fenn's illustration seems to show the ferry being pulled across hand-over-hand, a quite unlikely performance, while De Fontaine wrote:

"The ferry itself was antique and innocent of any but the rudest invention. It was cheap in construction, and the perfection of a simplicity that, so far as any improvement is concerned, might have originated among the antediluvians.

"A rope extending to some convenient tree on either bank; a flat-bottomed boat and a stout negro—that was the machinery. You drove down, whooped, received an answering yell, possessed your soul in patience until the return of the crazy craft, and entered cautiously. The cable passed through a guide-post attached to the gunwale, and the ferryman, seizing it with a peculiar wooden key, gave it a twist, and commenced the process of pulling his freight to the other side. If any thing gave way, as was not unfrequently the case during a freshet, you drifted helplessly down the current, with the chance of being poled ashore in some out-of-the-way spot, or of a cold bath in the river."

De Fontaine must have been an intolerant man, or accustomed more to the high road than the by-way, for the current ferry he found on the French Broad was, however crude, more substantial than some of the ferries still in use today. At about the same time O. B. Bunce came to Suck Creek, thirteen miles below Chattanooga, Tennessee, and wished to cross, ". . . but no means could be obtained to do so," he complained. "No boats were to be found along the shore excepting the primitive 'dug-out,' which every one said would not be safe on account of the swiftness and turbulence of the current. This was a little exasperating. The rudest savage tribes of the Pacific build canoes that can sail far out at sea in high winds and rough water, but the boats of the Tennessee can only be employed in the smoothest of water. They cannot be trusted in a ripple; and yet the very simple contrivance of an outrigger, such as used by the Pacific natives, would render them safe even in a high sea. The skill of our Tennessee men is equal, no doubt, to many emergencies of the mountains, but their resources for the water are certainly very limited . . ."

Though many people, like Cumings, have thought current ferries most ingenious, their invention was inescapable. They were known in Europe, but it is doubtful that American ferrymen were mere imitators. On the contrary, this is a tool which has been invented over and over again, at many times and many places, the product of need, of situation and of chance observation.

PICTURESQUE AMERICA, WILLIAM CULLEN BRYANT, ED., 1872

A ferry on the French Broad River in eastern Tennessee. The caption for this drawing by H. Fenn, which first appeared in William Cullen Bryant's *Picturesque America* (Appleton, 1872) said that "this crude ferry provided uncertain service to occasional travelers."

The need was for something larger than a canoe, a ferry large enough to carry horses, cattle and, later, wagons and coaches; the situation a common one in America: a river too deep to ford, too narrow for sailboats, and too swift for oarsmen.

The first innovation called for no great imagination: merely rigging a rope or cable across the stream to hold the flat against the current, with the intention, perhaps, that the lateral force would be applied by oars, or by pulling on the cable. Or there was another method, which was used in some places, such as at the Lehigh River ferry in Bethlehem, Pennsylvania, of tying a line to the ferry and having it pulled across by horses on shore, or by a windlass.

But the ferryman who sought to apply any of these methods had a surprise coming to him. The first time he found himself afloat, his flatboat held by the cable and, by chance, at an angle to the current, the boat would gently and smoothly drift across the stream without help!

Because of this, one cannot say with certainty when current ferries were introduced. That ferry on the Lehigh River, for example, was pulled by horses, according to one source; but another record refers to it as stream-propelled. Quite probably the operator discovered that stream force could replace his teams, so both references may be correct.

On the narrower streams, which could be spanned by rope, current ferries came into use almost as soon as flatboats were introduced to carry horses and, a little later, wagons. Known as "rope ferries," they worked very well, so long as the rope could be held above the water and not sag too much. The limits were broadened when wire cable could be procured, and in the early 1800's "wire ferries" spanned many rivers. Most of the Connecticut River ferries soon became wire ferries.

In the nineteenth century, wire ferries were set up throughout the Middle West, in the South, and beyond the Rockies, wherever rivers were suitable for their use and people had need to cross. They were inexpensive, simple, and easily operated. They were rapid enough to satisfy their users, and were certainly superior to oars or poles.

The wire made them relatively dependable, too. Rope, exposed to the elements, subjected to greater strain than its makers intended, and kept in service much too long, often broke. It snapped, usually, when the strain was heavy; as in spring freshets when the current was strong and the water turbulent. When it did break, passengers and ferryman could only hope, for there was no alternate security or power. The flatboat and all on board were carried downstream, and the best that was likely to happen was to drift to either shore, far below the landing place and the nearest road. At worst they might strike a rock or snag and capsize. More often than not the clumsy barge would hang up on a midstream shoal, leaving the passengers safe for the moment but helpless, the rushing waters separating them from both shores.

Technically, a ferry plies between fixed points, but before the current ferry came into use this was often true in only a general way. O. B. Bunce, telling of a crossing in Tennessee, about 1870, mentioned some of the difficulties at the landing:

"Arriving at the ferry near sunset, we experienced some amusing incidents in getting across the stream. It is one feature of this method of crossing a river that the exact place of landing cannot be controlled, the rise and fall of the stream varying it considerably. On our return we found the nose of the boat thrust into a bank, and some apprehensions prevailing as to how the waiting cargo was to be got on board. Our horses were unharnessed, and the vehicle, by the strenuous effort of half a dozen negroes, lifted on board. Then the horses, our own and several others, without much difficulty, jumped the space; but the cattle struggled, and backed, and plunged, with the most incorrigible perversity. Some charged back, and tried to escape up the hill; others plunged into the water; and one fine heifer was with difficulty saved from drowning. At last, after great effort, much shouting, and woeful confusion, cattle, horses, carriage, and pedestrians, were successfully

Georgia, 1941. Parks' Ferry, crossing the Oconee River, was still in use when this picture was taken in 1941, and it may still be. This is the simplest version of the current ferry. The angle of the boat is changed by means of the windlass. The operator, wearing a wool hat, is apparently trying to speed the pace of his leisurely craft.

shipped, but crowded together on the narrow flat with promiscuous disregard of class or species. . . ."

The early ferries—dugouts, canoes, bull-boats, keelboats, and other small craft—could usually be maneuvered to shore at any desired point. The point was in the general area of the "landing," but the ferryman chose the spot that seemed best at the moment. He might come in under an overhang, so passengers could step ashore, or in the lee of a point, or beside a convenient rock or log. The exact place would be changed as the water rose and fell, and in summer droughts he might have to lay a walkway of split logs and brush across mud flats to the nearest water. Often he would have one landing-place for human passengers, another for easier loading of cattle; or he might have to abandon one spot temporarily after it had been churned into mud by animal hooves.

Next to negligent service, high tolls, drunken ferrymen, unsafe craft, and too-intimate association with four-footed passengers, the traveler's most frequent complaint had to do with the condition of ferry landings. Local licensing authorities took this into account, and many ferry licenses were issued with the condition that the operator make suitable provision for his passengers to board the ferry dry-shod.

Where water-level fluctuated but little, wharves were built. Elsewhere the simplest solution was a flight of wooden steps or a ladder fixed to the wharf, or a set of stone steps built into the river bank.

This was good enough for people, and livestock could be herded aboard somehow. Loading a wagon was a more difficult proposition, however. The current ferry differed from free-floating craft in that it always returned to the same point; moving the landing up or downstream meant an hour or more of hard work. So now an improvement was needed. One could hardly keep ten able-bodied men at the landing to lift wagons aboard by main force, and it was absurd to spend hours unloading them, perhaps even dismantling them, merely to cross a river a hundred feet wide.

The improvement was a cobblestone ramp, built into the bank, sloping steeply enough so that the ferry could nose into it and a wooden platform be laid from the bow to shore, over which loaded wagons could be driven. It was not long before the wooden platform was permanently attached to the boat, pivoted and counter-weighted so it could be raised and lowered.

The floating bridge-dock was not used, as far as I can determine, until the 19th century. As a formal invention it is often credited to Robert Fulton. No doubt he perfected an elaboration of the idea, but the principle is so obvious it would be incredible had it not been used before.

A good wire ferry with good ramps and approaches offered the traveling public close to the maximum in service and convenience. Now vehicles could be driven aboard directly and driven off again on the other side. The ferry thus became, for the first time in full degree, "a floating section of highway." And the cable, fixing the landing-points, eliminated any doubts that the boat was, technically, a ferry, under the rigid terms laid down by New York attorney James McNamee in an 1887 legal brief: "The nature of a ferry is repugnant to indefiniteness in its termini . . ." The current ferry, by its very nature, and for the first time, set the modern pattern of a double-ended vessel.

The current ferry was almost the last word in short river crossings. Most of them have now been replaced by bridges. Seldom has a current ferry been replaced by a free-floating steamboat. The advantage gained would be too slight.

Many current ferries—just how many no one knows—continued in service well into the twentieth century. Between 1910 and 1920, for example, there were twenty or more in Oregon, most of them publicly operated.

Many are still in use, but one might not recognize them as such, because they have supplemental power plants. The development of small gasoline engines gave ferry operators a simple means of speeding the crossing, without investing in a fully-powered motor vessel.

A number of ingenious, home-grown rigs are in use. Usually the barge itself is unchanged; the engine is outboard. In some cases the engine is mounted in a fixed housing, from which propeller shafts run fore and aft, either of which can be engaged by a friction clutch; if one propeller is mounted backward, no reversing mechanism is needed. In other cases the entire engine housing is pivoted on the barge; stream-power moves the boat out of the slip, with sufficient speed to let the engine housing be swung around into driving position. (The accompanying picture shows a variation of this in a free-floating ferry, which has a tugboat pivoted to its side.)

A boat-propelled ferry. This picture, taken in 1938, shows the ferry crossing the Mississippi from New Madrid County in Missouri to the opposite shore in Tennessee, just below the Kentucky border. The launch in this picture is attached to the barge by bow pivot. It reverses engine to pull the barge from shore, then swings about to push it across the stream.

Still another power application was in use on a Wisconsin ferry which I saw in 1953; a steel cable passed from bank to bank, slackly enough to be submerged. As the ferry moved, this cable was picked up by pulleys fore and aft, and passed through another set of pulleys driven by a gasoline engine. Thus the boat pulled itself along the cable. A similar craft, the *Riverside* (but better known as the *Skillypot*), used to cross Rondout Creek between Kingston and Sleightsburg, New York, until 1923. Her donkey engine and windlass pulled up a lot of chain before the boat would start from the slip. There was a signal system rigged up to warn other craft when the slack in the cable was being taken up so they would not become fouled in it.

Should the reader see any ferry held in place by an overhead wire cable spanning the stream, he is looking at what is, potentially, a current ferry. Perhaps, as is often the case today, the operator no longer makes use of the free river power; he may prefer to operate the engine controls alone, not bothering to change the hull's angle to the stream on each crossing. But if by chance the engine should fail during the crossing, the passengers would not be unduly delayed. A few turns of a windlass would bring the boat into position, and she would complete her passage smoothly and silently.

When the first draft of this chapter was written, it contained the following statement: "Stream-power was used in Europe in a somewhat different way. 'Pendulum ferries' were in use on the Rhine in Germany, and on some rivers in southern Europe. No pendulum ferries are definitely known to have been established in America, though some say there was one on the Muskingum not far from Marietta."

I have never been able to pin down the facts on the Muskingum ferry. But before this book was completed, I bought a two-volume set of *Picturesque America*, edited by William Cullen Bryant and published by D. Appleton & Company in 1872. My quotations from De Fontaine and Bunce were drawn from the volumes, as were Harry Fenn's illustrations.

It was this second Fenn illustration we show here that puzzled me, and I thought at first, mistakenly, that the series of platforms carrying masts were intended to support a cable which spanned the stream, for they seem to be in line with the far shore. But a moment's study showed that this could not be the case, for there is no visible connection with the near shore.

Bunce's explanation settled it: I had found a real pendulum ferry:

"It is a rope-ferry, having for motive power the river-current, which it masters for its purpose by a very simple application of a law in physics. A long rope from the ferry-boat, supported at regular intervals on poles resting on small flat-boats, is attached, several hundred feet up-stream, to an island in mid-water. The boat thus secured is pushed from the shore, when it begins to catch the force of the

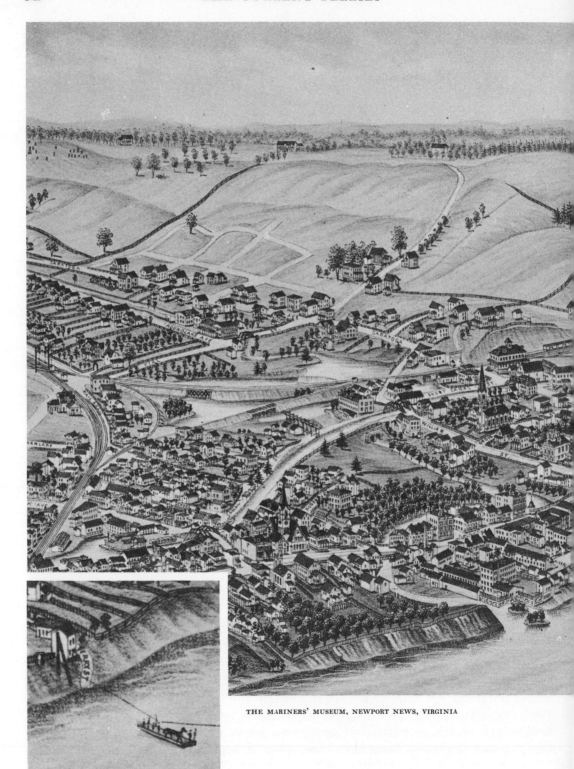

THE MARINERS' MUSEUM, NEWPORT NEWS, VIRGINIA

Mechanicville, New York, in 1884. Note the numerous rail lines and the canal with horse-drawn canal boats. A current ferry is crossing the Hudson. Mechanicville is some miles above Albany, where large ships can go, and above the confluence of the Mohawk and the Erie Barge Canal with the Hudson, so there was no difficulty about the ferry cable interfering with river traffic.

current, a greater surface of pressure being secured by a board, like the center-board of a sail-boat, which is dropped down deep into the water on the upper side. The current sweeping against the boat would carry it downstream, but the attached rope retains the vessel in place, and we have, as a result of the sum of the forces, the boat swiftly propelled on the arc of a circle across the stream. Thus, by a very simple contrivance, a motor is secured which requires neither fuel nor canvas, which is uniformly available, and which is obtained entirely without cost. A very odd effect in the scene is the fleet of small flat-boats, upholding the long and heavy rope, which start in company with the large vessel in the order and with the precision of a column of cavalry. Moving in obedience to no visible sign or force, they impress one as being the intelligent directors of the movement . . ."

Bunce says that the pendulum ferry was "occasionally" found in the South, but until some local historian offers other examples, this one near Chattanooga can enjoy the distinction of uniqueness.

A fascinating question remains: How did this pendulum ferry happen to be there? The need existed, to be sure; the bridge at Chattanooga had washed out a few years before Bunce's visit and had not been replaced, and the river here is too wide for a rope or wire ferry. But accidental discovery of the pendulum-ferry principle is much less likely than stumbling on the rope ferry. True, any competent physicist of the time could have designed a pendulum ferry. But the makeshift, ramshackle apparatus sketched by Fenn is hardly suggestive of scientific parentage.

PICTURESQUE AMERICA, WILLIAM CULLEN BRYANT, ED., 1872

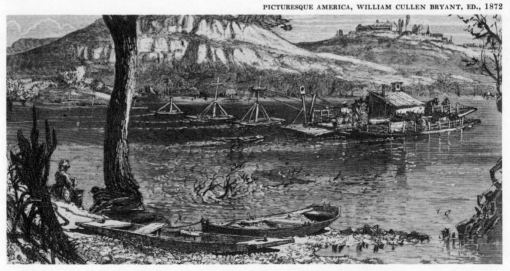

A pendulum ferry, 1870. Bryant wrote that "this ferry, at Chattanooga, Tennessee, is the only one of its kind found by the author. A rope from the ferry is supported by small flat-boats and anchored to an island midstream. A centerboard and sweeps, placed at an angle to the current, cause the boat to traverse an arc from shore to shore."

Floating Horsepower

CHAPTER SEVEN

CURRENT FERRIES WERE a wonderful solution for crossing such narrow streams as the Connecticut, the Muskingum, and the North Platte. But there could be no such device for crossing the broad Missouri, or at tidewater, as between Brooklyn and Manhattan. That there was such an elegant solution elsewhere, however, may have aggravated an already irked Brooklyn populace.

Public dissatisfaction with the Brooklyn ferries was mounting month by month. The city was growing, commerce leaping ahead. By 1800 editorial writers were remarking upon the age of invention which America had entered. Improvements were everywhere, except in the ferries, and the sailing periauger was as dangerous and unreliable as ever. Brooklynites took out their tempers on the ferrymen, often with good reason, but sometimes because they had no better target.

One oft-embroiled ferryman was James Harding, favored by the New York Corporation but not as well regarded by the Brooklynites he served. One dissatisfied customer was a butcher, William Webbing, who poured out his complaints in a lawsuit in pre-Revolutionary days, averring:

". . . That he has received many abuses of late from James Harding, the ferryman, not only by abusive words, but several times by his carelessness had had his creatures destroyed and killed in bringing from the ferry to New York; the particulars of which would be too tedious to trouble this honorable court with all, and therefore your petitioner will confine himself with what hath been transacted by said Mr. Harding, since the 26th of this instant, month of July, on which day, about noon, your petitioner had *two* cattle brought to the ferry, and put into the common pen or yard where cattle always used to be put, in order to be brought over to the slaughter house in New York; on which day, in the afternoon, your

55

petitioner went over to said Harding, *and treated him handsomely*, and prayed him to bring said two cattle over by the first opportunity, which he said should be done; but said cattle not being brought over, according to expectation, on Friday the 28th instant, your petitioner went over again, to know what was the reason said cattle were not brought over *in four high waters*, at a time of calm good weather, and when your petitioner came, the said Harding told him he could not carry them now, nor could he tell when they could be carried over, so that your petitioner was forced to turn said cattle into a pasture after they had stood standing in a pen for the space of *four high tides*, during which time your petitioner had no beef for the market but what he borrowed, and when your petitioner expostulated with this ferryman about his neglect therein, his answer was that Jeremiah Calcutt was dead, and that he would make all the butchers in New York *truckle* to him before Christmas, nor would he bring said cattle over, unless your petitioner would come over and help to load them . . .”

A frequent source of minor disturbances was a colorful and somewhat eccentric Brooklynite named Diana Rapalje, who died at the age of 82 in 1849. A correspondent to the New York *Evening Post* later recalled some of Miss Rapalje’s contributions to the general liveliness on board:

“Once, in crossing the Brooklyn Ferry, some ladies were excessively startled and sprang from their seats in frightful apprehension. A snake was seen wriggling on the floor. Diana witnessed their alarm with supreme contempt and soon relieved it. ‘It is only one of my eels,’ said she, pulling some others from her pocket, which she had bought in Fly Market, and whose comrade was attempting an escape. It is needless to say she restored him to her eelymosynary receptacle.

“At another time the clarion tones of chanticleer came from the bosom of the same dignified lady sitting smoothly erect in the same cabin. Lest people might suppose she was exercising her own lungs upon the chromatic scale, she opened her shawl and exposed a roystering bird of the genus rooster, which she informed the company was intended for chicken soup.”

While people often complained about the ferrymen, more than once the latter had occasion to feel put upon. Certainly this was true of Timothy Crady and Thomas Burk, the ferrymen unlucky enough to be on duty one day in 1795, when a self-important New York politician descended the ferry stairs in Brooklyn.

Gabriel Furman, Alderman of the First Ward, felt that his exalted position carried with it certain special prerogatives, for no sooner did he reach the landing than he ordered Crady and Burk to take him across. Unimpressed, they refused to leave before the scheduled time, preferring to have more than one fare for their trouble.

By departure time the men were not on the best of terms, and they continued to argue on the way across the East River, until Furman threatened to have both ferrymen arrested and Crady replied that he'd put a boat hook through the first man to lay a hand on him.

Furman's threat was more heartfelt than Crady's, for soon after they landed in New York he prevailed upon an officer of the law to come to the landing and arrest both Burk and Crady. He followed the prisoners to jail, poking them in the back with his cane and promising them rough treatment.

This they got. They were held in prison for two weeks before the Bridewell court heard their case. Both men were convicted; Burk was sentenced to two months in jail, Crady to two months, plus twenty lashes.

The Bridewell court was already infamous, and this new case stirred citizens to angry condemnation. William Kettletas was among them, and he wrote numerous letters to the press, pointing out, among other things, that the court included three of Furman's fellow aldermen. Demands were made that the court modify its sentence, and when the court refused the legislature was petitioned to impeach the court. The legislators declined. Kettletas denounced them for their inaction, and they adopted a resolution demanding that he apologize. He declined to do so and was promptly hurled into the same prison as the ferrymen.

He kept up his campaign from his cell and was the first to report that Crady was dead, apparently of complications caused by the twenty lashes. When the legislature adjourned a few days later, a court order freed Kettletas, and cheering citizens greeted him at the prison gate. On Burk's behalf he filed suit against the Bridewell court, and Burk was awarded $500 in redress. Nothing could be done for Crady.

There were complaints about ferry service, ferry rates, monopolies, and other matters, but the roots of dissatisfaction were deeper. Each winter had its toll of tragedies, for to capsize in icy water meant almost certain death. The year around there were delays; in stormy weather or in dead calms New York butchers might be cut off from their supply of meat for days at a time. No one would insure ferry-borne animals, and with good reason: the stoutest vessel in use could be swamped or capsized if cattle panicked and plunged to one side.

It is a curious fact that two answers should be brought forward at about the same time: the teamboat and the steamboat. The steamboat was a major scientific achievement, a successful inventive application of new discoveries in basic science. The teamboat, on the other hand, was a very old idea—if the accompanying drawing is to be credited. It was little more than a variation of animal-powered devices used in many parts of the world for centuries.

Naming the "first" teamboat to provide ferry service in America is another risky declaration, as open to challenge as some of the other "first" nominations. In this case another hazard in the interpretation of old records is their inconsistent

Philadelphia, about 1820. At the right is the Cooper's Point ferry
house and tavern at Camden, New Jersey. From here the stagecoach
left for New York. At this time the journey required two days.
At the wharf is a teamboat, propelled by horses on a treadmill. A

econd teamboat is rounding the upper end of Windmill Island,
hrough which a channel was cut in later years. The tallest steeple
n this view belongs to Christ Church, that farthest to the left be-
ongs to Swedes Church, built in 1677.

nomenclature. What they called a "horse boat," was, in some cases, a ferry built *to carry* horses; in others it was a ferry *propelled* by horses. Before 1814, because of its novelty, horse propulsion would not have been passed by without comment. So it is likely that the "horse boats" prior to this date were all or nearly all horse-carrying boats.

HARPER'S NEW MONTHLY MAGAZINE, FEBRUARY, 1872

A Roman ox-boat. The horse-propelled teamboat was, supposedly, invented early in the nineteenth century. But a book whose Latin title is too long to reproduce here, published in Basle, Switzerland, in 1552, contained this illustration. The text described the boat as an early Roman war vessel, propelled by oxen.

In 1814 what may have been the first horse-propelled boat went into service on the Catherine Street run between Brooklyn and Manhattan. This was seven years after Fulton's *Clermont* steamed up the Hudson. A few other steamboats were in use, but the steamboat was, as yet, unproven. The residents of Brooklyn hailed the teamboat joyously, for it was a tremendous improvement over anything they had known.

To be sure, Robert Fulton and William Cutting had already formed the New York and Brooklyn Steamboat Ferry Associates, a lease had been given them, and other ferry operators had been told they should be prepared to go out of business as soon as the steam ferries were ready. But they were not ready, and many Brooklynites doubted that they ever would be. Further, Fulton and Cutting had won, in advance, the right to double ferry tolls, and Brooklyn citizens, far from greeting the steamboat era with gladness, had held a protest meeting.

The teamboat, which came to have a number of shapes and forms, was essentially a barge equipped with paddle wheels, which were driven by horses walking on a treadmill or around a capstan. The one fact which makes suspect the claim of a "first" for the Catherine Street boat is its size: Ordinarily a new idea is tested first on a modest scale, but this one was almost the largest ever built, and it was highly successful.

The Long Island *Star* said Moses Rogers built this teamboat. It was driven by eight horses walking on treadmills. On its first full day of service, it crossed the river twelve times, taking from 8 to 18 minutes per trip, carrying an average of 200 passengers plus horses and vehicles. On a single trip, several days later, it carried 543 passengers.

For the much-abused commuters who had enjoyed nothing larger, safer or more dependable than the periauger, the horse boat was marvelous indeed. A second one was launched in June 1814, and the New York *Columbian* reported:

"This morning was launched, at the shipyard of Mr. Charles Browne, an elegant double boat, intended to ply as a ferry from Corlaers Hook to Williamsburgh, Long Island. This beautiful boat is called the *Williamsburgh,* and is to be propelled by horse-power, with machinery very different from that already constructed and used in the Hoboken or Brooklyn boats, and is thought by competent judges to be very complete . . ."

This news story casts a shadow over the "first" claim for Catherine Street, for it mentions that a Hoboken horse boat was already in operation in June, 1814. This information conflicts also with Hoboken histories, which state that Stevens proposed to introduce horse boats in 1813, but did not actually do so until 1815. Since, according to this report, his horse boat was operating before June, 1814, it may actually have preceded the Catherine Street horse-driven ferry.

A few months after the horse-boat ferry began regular service, the Fulton-Cutting steamboat ferry *Nassau* was ready. The Brooklyn sceptics soon became enthusiasts, for she was even larger and swifter than the horse boat, and apparently even safer. She was easy to load and unload, and on one of the first Sundays of her career she made forty crossings. The Long Island *Star* editorialized:

"This is a refinement, a *luxury* of pleasure unknown to the old world . . . The captain, lordly as old Neptune, drives his splendid car regardless of wind or tide, and is able to tell with certainty the hour of his return . . ."

The horse-boat ferry was introduced too late to have an era all its own. But for two decades the horse boat led the steam ferry by a wide margin. Even Fulton's

NEW YORK PUBLIC LIBRARY, PHELPS STOKES COLLECTION

Hartford, on the Connecticut, 1840. Sail still predominated, but steamers were beginning to appear on the river. The ferry at center appears to be a teamboat.

successors—he died in 1815—were in no hurry to put steamboats in use. They were under contract to add a second steam ferry on the Brooklyn run, as a condition of their lease, but they tried to wriggle out of the commitment, offering to add a horse boat a year sooner. And they supported their (unsuccessful) plea by declaring that teamboats were safer than steamboats and easier to navigate!

On the other side of Manhattan, Colonel John Stevens' teamboat was just as successful. It, too, was large, consisting of three hulls, each ninety feet long, fastened together, with space between for the paddle wheels. At the center was a circular platform, with cleats for footholds, on which the horses walked. Two horses might propel the boat in a calm, if it were lightly loaded, but there was room for eight. Mules were used for a time.

Stevens was a rival of Robert Fulton in steamboat development, and he had already built some steamboats before entering the ferry business. But Fulton and his associate, Robert R. Livingston, had obtained a legal monopoly of steam navigation in the waters around New York State, and Stevens was not just then prepared to challenge them.

The visitor to present-day Hoboken may be incredulous to hear that it was once a pleasure resort, but so it was. In 1663 Nicholas Varlett obtained a patent for the bouwerie of Hoboken, 276 acres of land on the New Jersey shore, directly across from Manhattan Island. Title changed hands several times, until some time before the American Revolution, when William Bayard acquired it.

Bayard sought to realize some income from his landholdings, and he decided to offer New Yorkers a better way to cross the river. First he built an inn and then he prompted Cornelius Haring to enter the ferrying business. Haring inserted this advertisement in the New York *Journal* one day in 1775:

> Cornelius Haring, Presents his most respectful compliments to the Public, and informs them that on Monday the first of May, he opened the New Established Ferry from the remarkable, pleasant and convenient situated place of William Bayard, Esq., at Hoebuck from which place all Gentlemen Travelers and others—who have occasion to cross that ferry will be accomodated with the best of boats of every kind suitable to the wind and weather . . . The boats are to be distinguished by the name HOBOOCK FERRY painted on their stern.

Haring's ferry naturally came under military control during the war which burst so shortly thereafter. After the war Bayard, loyal to the King, lost his holdings, which in turn were acquired by Colonel Stevens. But Stevens didn't get the ferry rights, and there was no authority on the Jersey side potent enough to challenge the New York Common Council, which was chartering the Hudson River ferries. The Council leased Haring's old Hoboken ferry to John Van Alen. Finally, in 1789 Stevens bid successfully for a three-year lease, but this was not renewed.

Stevens probably was not overly concerned; just so long as the ferry was well operated, it would promote the value of his Hoboken properties.

First and foremost Stevens was an inventor. From 1789 onward his dominating interest was the development of steam engines and their application to land and water transportation. When legal and technical barriers hampered his exploitation of the steamboat, however, he turned to the teamboat as the best available means of linking Hoboken to New York. This, in due course, embroiled him with one Philip Hone, who, among other distinctions, was Mayor of New York.

Just how this came about is too tangled a story to be told here, even if one were able to resolve the wild confusion and conflict among the existing records and accounts. Apparently Stevens sold his ferry lease to John, Robert, and Samuel Swartwouts (or Swarthout). Either they, in turn, sold the lease to Hone, or the New York Ferry Committee took it up for non-payment of rent and transferred it to Hone. This happened in 1818, at the same time the New York terminal was moved from Murray to Barclay Street, where the Hoboken Ferry lands today. Hone operated at least one horse boat on this run; and the following year he obtained a lease for a new line between Hoboken and Christopher Street, Manhattan, a ferry service maintained until March 1955.

What irked Stevens, apparently, was the quality of Hone's service to Hoboken-bound passengers, one of whom published his complaints in a broadside.

"We embarked upon an aquatic conveyance called by the people of these parts a horse boat. But I am inclined to believe that this novelty is a mere sham, a trick upon travellers.

"There are a dozen sorry nags in this contrivance, which go round in a circular walk with halters on one end and beams at the other extremity. How this orbicular movement can promote the rectilinear advancement of this mammoth boat is to me a mystery. And as we were six hours in crossing the river, I suspect that they go and come with the tide and that the horses are a mere catch-penny to bring their masters the trigesimoseccundal part of a dollar more on every head than the customary ferriage . . ."

Hone is said to have been something of a socialist, but his sympathies did not extend to four-footed creatures, according to Stevens, who claimed that crippled horses and mules were made to work in harness from sunrise to sunset. And, having penned up his passengers in mid-river for hours at a time, Hone provided his boats with bars, thus robbing Stevens' pub of its trade. And, finally, Hone refused to provide service after sundown, cutting Stevens off from the profitable after-dark trade.

Finally Stevens brought suit against Hone, on the grounds that his terms of sale to the Swartwouts included a proviso that they not re-sell. Hone finally settled out of court; Stevens and his sons reacquired the ferry rights; the Hoboken Steamboat Ferry Company was incorporated in 1821; and in 1822, when the steam ferry *Hoboken* was put in service, the teamboat was finished in the New York City area. On the Brooklyn side, teamboats were being converted to steam.

After 1814, teamboats were adopted rapidly in many parts of the country. There was one over the Hudson at Newburgh in 1816, where a ferry still operates.

Cassville, Wisconsin in 1829. This view, and the two succeeding, show three stages in the evolution of a ferry. This view shows the landing, but it is not clear whether or not the two small boats shown are in ferry service. Note the man poling the furthermost boat through the shallow water. The river is the Mississippi; the opposite shore belongs to Iowa.

Another was introduced at Crawlier's Ferry on the Hudson, at Douw's Point, near which Captain Kidd supposedly buried treasure. By 1819 the teamboat had reached the Ohio, for in that year a large one, propelled by eight horses, was in service at Maysville, Kentucky.

In 1832 a traveler mentioned a four-horse teamboat on the Ohio at Wheeling, West Virginia, and another on the Missouri at St. Charles, northwest of St. Louis. In 1838 the Wisconsin Territorial authorities granted a ferry license for Prairie du Chien, where the first boat was mule-powered. Another was authorized at Cass-

After a time the teamboat came to Cassville. This is an excellent view of such a craft, showing the two horses in their stalls and the paddlewheels which were turned by the horses on the treadmill. This picture may have been taken in the late nineteenth century or early in the twentieth.

ville and a photograph of that one appears in this book. Indeed, as late as 1850 new teamboats were being put into service in the Middle West.

Another reference, undated but not much earlier than 1855, had this to say of the Leavenworth, Kansas, Ferry: "We crossed the Missouri River on a ferry called the old horse boat. This was run by a Mr. Yoakum and the motive power was a pair of horses that worked on a treadmill. Ice chunks were floating in the river that day, making the crossing very dangerous. Leavenworth did not amount to much then . . ."

One final photograph ends the teamboat story in a tantalizing way. I found it in the Bettman Archive in New York. Pasted to it was this typed caption:

"A Curious Coincidence: An American machine to which a parallel was found by the Peking-Paris Motorists in Central Asia. The subject of the photograph is

the last horse-ferry on the Mississippi. The raft is propelled by stern-wheel paddles driven by horse-power, the horses pulling levers on the deck exactly like the
old-fashioned Scotch threshing-mill. The Peking-Paris Motorists found a similar
machine in use in Central Asia."

That is all, except to note that the "horses" are mules, and the photograph
is heavily retouched. There is no identification. The Bettmann Archive has no idea
where the photograph came from. So, unless some reader can contribute a fact,
the time and place of the "last horse-ferry on the Mississippi" will remain a
mystery.

STATE HISTORICAL SOCIETY, WISCONSIN

Mechanical power finally arrives. This is a 1915 picture of a gasoline-driven ferry at Cassville. Though motor-driven the craft is
still paddle-propelled.

Prairie du Chien, Wisconsin, 1830. About thirty miles north on the Mississippi from Cassville, this crossing was soon to become a major link in the eastward transportation of crops from Iowa and Minnesota. The view is from the Iowa shore.

Bellevue, Iowa. The Mississippi River steamer in the background
suggests that this German lithograph should be dated about 1840.
There is a ferry in the foreground, just behind the second tree from
the right. The man with the whip, the shed, and the wheel housings
indicate that this was a teamboat. The view is from the Illinois
shore.

THE BETTMAN ARCHIVE

Last of the tribe? This photograph, source and date unknown, shows "the last horse ferry on the Mississippi." Though much more recent than the teamboats of the early nineteenth century, it is far cruder and smaller. Notice the long steering oar.

Devil in a Sawmill

CHAPTER EIGHT

LIKE MANY ANOTHER YOUNG LAD, I was taught that James Watt invented the steam engine after watching a tea kettle in his mother's kitchen, and that Robert Fulton invented the steamboat. The real-life story is not so neat. James Watt, to begin with, was more scientist than inventor; he did not "invent" the steam engine, but what he did was far more significant.

He was an instrument-maker at the University of Glasgow, a friend and associate of Europe's outstanding scientists in a period of great scientific fertility, and a leading advocate of metric measurement. His interest in the steam engine was stimulated when a model of one was brought to him for repair.

This engine, the Newcomen, was operated by steam, but on a principle quite different from that of post-Watt engines. Steam was introduced into a cylinder below the piston and the port closed; the cylinder was then cooled, causing the steam to condense and the pressure within the cylinder to drop below atmospheric pressure. The other end of the cylinder being open, atmospheric pressure pushed the piston downward. The Newcomen engine, an example of which can be seen in the Henry Ford Museum at Dearborn, Michigan, was huge and cumbersome in relation to its small power output, and its only significant use had been to pump water from mine shafts.

Watt, by a brilliant analysis of heat mechanics, applied steam as a positive source of power. Having first applied steam at one end of a piston in a closed cylinder, he later developed the double-acting engine. Step by step he gave the steam engine its basic scientific design, and, in partnership with Matthew Boulton, patented and built steam engines which inaugurated the age of power.

Watt's principal work was done in the fifteen years between 1769 and 1784. By the end of that period, inventors, gadgeteers, engineers, and mechanics in

Europe and America were in a ferment of creativeness, proposing to apply steam power in a wild diversity of ways, from flying machines to terrible engines of war.

One of the most obvious applications of steam power was to some kind of boat, and it was thus applied before any land vehicle was steam-driven. But who invented

Newcomen's steam engine.

HARPER'S NEW MONTHLY MAGAZINE

the steamboat? Not Robert Fulton, for he saw Symington's *Charlotte Dundas* in England well before his own first attempt to build one. More than a dozen men are credited with being "first," and at least three nations, France, England, and the United States, are believed—but to a large extent only within their own borders—to deserve the honors of priority. A writer in *Harper's New Monthly Magazine* stated the case in 1876 as well as it has ever been done:

"The truth is, the engine was Newcomen's, and then Watt's, and the boat was any body's; and persons went to work here and there, with varying degrees of success, depending upon political influence, social standing, moneyed resources, or friends thus provided, and last, not least, mechanical talent for harnessing the engine to the paddle or propeller used to push against the water."

I will not attempt here to do justice to the British, Scotch, or French claims. Or to the German and Russian either, for they are not adequately represented in American literature. The American story is complex enough, and it begins with James Rumsey and John Fitch.

Rumsey, except for the fact that he lived in Maryland, fits neatly into the character of "Yankee inventor." He had little schooling; he worked for a time as a blacksmith; in 1782, at age 39, he was part owner of a grist mill at Sleepy Creek, Maryland. But the mill failed because Rumsey pursued his dreams instead of minding his business. Moving to a popular resort in western Virginia, he made the acquaintance of George Washington while building a house and stable for him, and when his debts made it expedient for him to move again, Washington gave him a job as construction superintendent for the Potomac Navigation Company, of which Washington was president. But he quit after only a year.

Rumsey was working secretly on *something* as early as 1783. In seeking capital, he called it a "mechanically-propelled boat," not steam-propelled. His admirers and supporters, who later founded the Rumseian Society to promote his ventures, said he was thinking about steam propulsion then, but even they conceded that his actual experiments with steam didn't begin until 1785. He is said to have captured Washington's interest by demonstrating his mechanical boat for him in 1784, and with the General's encouragement he built one steamboat which was destroyed by fire. Then he built another which he launched at Sir John's Run on the Potomac in 1785 and brought downstream to Harper's Ferry, where he continued experiments.

All of this, however, was in secret, and before Rumsey showed anything publicly, John Fitch had tested his steamboat on the Delaware in 1786. Fitch's test was well publicized, and Rumsey's backers, including Washington, now insisted that he, too, make a public showing. He did so, but at this point authorities disagree. All agree that he did successfully demonstrate a steamboat, and that the demonstration was on the Potomac at Shepherdstown, Virginia. But some say it was in 1786, a few months after Fitch's demonstration, while others make it 1787, over a year later.

Fitch, in any event, got the better publicity, and Rumsey, unable to find financial backing, went to England. He obtained English patents, and, finally, American patents, too. A second steamboat, the *Columbia Maid*, was nearing completion when he died in London in 1792.

John Fitch had persuaded the New Jersey legislature to grant him a 15-year monopoly in the use of steamboats before he had actually built any. The steamer he tested on the Delaware in the summer of 1786 impressed the public, in part because of its fantastic appearance, and in part because it really worked, but no one, including Fitch, considered it a practical vessel. He built two more, making considerable progress, and then a fourth, which he operated commercially. It provided a scheduled passenger and freight service on the Delaware and Schuylkill rivers. Shortly thereafter the legislatures of several states, including Pennsylvania and New York, followed New Jersey's lead in granting Fitch exclusive rights to steam navigation on their rivers.

Fitch's next demonstration was on Collect Pond, Manhattan, in 1796, but in the meantime other steamboat builders had made their offerings. Nathan Reed of Massachusetts put a steam-propelled paddle boat in service between Beverly and Danvers in 1789. Reed's may have been the first American steam ferryboat, for Fitch's Delaware-Schuylkill operation was river service rather than ferrying.

Elijah Ormsbee, at Pawtucket in 1792, came forward with a steam vessel armed with goosefoot paddles, similar to those used by Fitch, which imitated a rowing action. And another Yankee, Captain Samuel Morey of Fairlee, Vermont, had a steam-driven boat on the Connecticut River in 1793.

John Stevens of Hoboken was probably the best-qualified of the Americans who tried to build steamboats. He was well-educated, a good engineer and designer, serious-minded, hardly the kind who anticipates fame and fortune through a single intuitive conception. His attention was attracted to steamboats by the work of Rumsey and Fitch, and he began his experiments about 1789. In February of that year he asked that the New York legislature grant him the exclusive privilege of building steamboats, but having already granted that privilege to John Fitch, the legislature declined. As an alternative, he helped promote a federal patent law, and he soon had patents on an improved vertical steam boiler, an improved steam engine, an application of steam to the working of bellows, and an application of the steam engine to a boat with paddle wheels.

His father's death burdened him with numerous business chores, but what delayed his progress even more was the difficulty of building the devices he conceived. He himself was neither machinist nor mechanic, and workmen with the needed skills were rare.

About 1797 he had a fortunate meeting with Nicholas J. Roosevelt, who had an interest in a foundry and, best of all, had in his employ several skilled workmen recently arrived from England. Roosevelt became Stevens' associate, and Stevens also interested his brother-in-law, Robert R. Livingston, and the three men signed a 20-year compact in 1800.

Livingston's role was somewhat extraordinary. A member of the Continental Congress, he was one of the committee that drafted the Constitution of the United States, and one of a group that wrote the New York State constitution. He administered the first Presidential oath to George Washington in 1789 and negotiated the Louisiana Purchase in 1803.

John Fitch's New York monopoly lapsed when he failed to produce a successful steamboat for use on the waters of that state, and Livingston, though no inventor himself, had the legislature transfer the grant to himself in 1798. This would give him the exclusive right to navigate all boats driven by "fire or steam" in New York waters for twenty years—provided he built a successful boat within one year. He didn't, but by skillful maneuvering was able to keep the grant alive.

Livingston controlled this grant personally. He did not make it an asset of the Stevens-Roosevelt-Livingston enterprise. Thus he was free to talk business with Robert Fulton in Paris when the two men met there in 1803. Fulton, too, was interested in steamboats. He had seen Symington's operating on the Forth and Clyde Canal. Symington's boat was powered with a Watt double-acting engine working by a connecting-rod to a crank on a paddle-wheel shaft, the first known example of steam power being applied in this way.

If the *Charlotte Dundas* could have been sailed to New York, she might have qualified under the terms of the New York legislature's grant. But this was impossible, so Livingston and Fulton had a clear field. Fulton tested a steamboat on the Seine in 1803, but it was a failure. Livingston was not dismayed. He continued to finance Fulton's work in New York, while at the same time he continued his relationships with Stevens.

Stevens actually operated an experimental steamboat on the Passaic River in New Jersey in 1798. In 1804, the year after Fulton's failure in France, Stevens' *Little Juliana* steamed across the Hudson and back. Neither boat was designed for commercial service, but the *Little Juliana's* performance was good enough to encourage Stevens to go ahead with a full-scale vessel. The *Little Juliana* was driven by a Watt engine; the boiler was built to Stevens' own design; and she had a bladed screw-propeller.

In that same year, 1804, Oliver Evans was testing a stern-paddle-wheel steamboat on the Schuylkill and Delaware rivers. It had two unique characteristics: first, a high-pressure steam engine which was the first of its kind; second, wheels designed to propel the boat either in the water or on land.

Stevens' 100-foot *Phoenix* was nearing completion when Robert Fulton sailed the *Clermont* up the Hudson in 1807.

The *Clermont* was not a pure steamboat; she had masts and sails as well. Fulton claimed in his patent application that this was an advantage, and that he was first to demonstrate "the utility of the union of the two powers of wind and steam." Her engine came from the shops of Boulton and Watt; Fulton had bought it when he was in England. Her hull came from the Brooklyn shipyard of Charles Browne, who also built several teamboats.

So one may question the magnitude of Fulton's achievement. He did invent the outside bearing of the paddle-wheel shaft, and some of the mechanical linkages were undoubtedly his, though they generally followed Symington's design. The *Clermont* was far from being the first steamboat; at least fifteen and probably more than twenty had been built earlier.

But there is no question but that the *Clermont* was the first practical, operating commercial steamboat in American waters. She was a vessel of 160 tons, designed to carry both passengers and cargo. The New York legislature had granted the monopoly on condition that the vessel cruise at 4 miles per hour. On her first Hudson voyage the *Clermont* did 5 miles per hour. She stopped overnight at Livingston's estate, for which she was named; and it was on this voyage that, according to legend, a farmer spied her and ran off to say he "had seen the devil going up the river in a sawmill." When she arrived back in New York, the monopoly had been won, the press was full of her achievement, and the day was Robert Fulton's.

Now the legislature added a bonus, at Livingston's wish. The monopoly would be extended five years for each new steamboat he put in service!

When the story of the steamboat is told to children, it often stops here, as if, after this one voyage, the steamboat became standard and commonplace. But the fact is that nothing much changed, other than incentive. If anything, the *Clermont's* voyage slowed the development of steam navigation, because of the monopoly. The basic mechanical problems were still the same, and the *Clermont* symbolized only one step in the long process of their solution.

One could buy a steam engine in England and have a hull built in America. But constructing the machinery to deliver the power to a paddle-wheel, or even building a good paddle-wheel, was beyond the skill of most American mechanics. Before steam there had never been occasion to build a boiler or form tubing or make joints capable of withstanding high internal pressures. Much had to be learned, and the only available teacher was failure.

Failure was more common in the early steamers than success, and failure could mean a violent end to the engineer and his ship. If steamboats were to become heavier and faster than they were, both temperatures and pressures would have to go higher and higher. The only way to find whether a boiler would contain these higher pressures and temperatures was to try it. In consequence boiler explosions were appallingly frequent.

Danger or not, the *Clermont* was an overnight success. Thirty-two hours to Albany! It was faster and more comfortable than a journey by horseback, stagecoach, or sloop. Rivermen immediately recognized in the *Clermont* a threat to their way of life and they took steps to quash that threat. They cut across her bows, they tried to force her aground, they even tried to sink her by ramming. But the ever-cooperative New York legislature promptly passed a law making it a crime willfully to injure a steamboat. After a year or so Fulton sent the *Clermont* to the shipyard for refitting and enlargement, and he changed her name to *North River*.

Fulton's success was no balm to Stevens' heart, for his *Phoenix* was completed and ready to go in 1808. He would have liked to put her in ferry service between Hoboken and New York, but he was blocked by the Livingston-Fulton monopoly. Unable to use his boat in New York waters, Stevens turned her over to his sons, who sailed her to Philadelphia, a voyage which made the *Phoenix* the first American-built steam vessel to sail the open sea. By 1809 she was running on the Delaware between Trenton and Philadelphia, a link in the stagecoach route from New York.

The following year Stevens obtained a ferry license from New York city authorities, which included a provision that he put a steamboat on the run. He wrote to Fulton about this, saying he was willing "to make you any compensation you desire for your patent, right, etc." And though they failed to reach agreement, in September, 1811, Stevens brought forth the *Juliana*. She was the first steam ferry in New York waters, and a highly successful boat. She was fast, making sixteen round trips in a day, carrying a hundred passengers or more on each trip.

Here was an open challenge to the monopoly, and the Fulton group was quick to take it up.

THE STEVENS INSTITUTE OF TECHNOLOGY

John Stevens' *Little Juliana,* many years after her first trip across the Hudson. Originally driven by a single screw, she was later fitted with two, which are faintly visible in the lower left hand corner of this picture. Note broad, comfortable lines, date on the stern.

Justice Marshall Steps In: Gibbons vs. Ogden

~~~~~~

CHAPTER NINE

THE PATENT LAW of the United States provides that the author of an invention shall be given an exclusive right to its use over a period of years. Within that period he can do as he wishes: he can sell his patent or issue licenses for others to make use of; he can retain a monopoly of its use; or he can suppress it. This is considered a just reward for invention. But more than that, it is a needed incentive, for without patent protection an inventor might spend a large sum in developing a device, only to have others appropriate it cost-free.

Congress had enacted a patent law by 1800, but the degree of protection this afforded was as yet uncertain. Nor was it clear that patent protection alone would give Livingston and Fulton the assurance they wished. The patent law was federal, and the definition of federal powers and their relation to the powers of the several states was incomplete. Coastal and river navigation had been largely unregulated up to then, and ferry charters had been issued by territories, states, counties, and municipalities.

So it was not altogether unreasonable for John Fitch, in the first instance, to seek and the New York legislature to grant another kind of protection. If he built a successful steamboat within a stipulated period, he would have the exclusive right to exploit steam navigation in New York waters for a period of years. He failed; Livingston obtained a similar grant, and with Fulton he succeeded.

The monopoly might have run its course unchallenged had the land on both sides of the Hudson been New York. But the western shore, opposite New York City was New Jersey, and so there was once again the conflict of jurisdiction which had entangled the Philadelphia and Brooklyn ferries before the Revolution. With Fulton as New York's cause and Stevens as New Jersey's, there began a battle of legal and legislative strategies.

The New York legislature supported its monopoly by the claim that; under a royal grant, New York's jurisdiction extended to the high-water mark on the New Jersey side, thus including the entire river. There was nothing unusual in such a situation; the District of Columbia extends across the Potomac River to the high-water mark on the Virginia shore. But New Jersey rejected the New York claim, and its legislature asserted that New Jersey's jurisdiction extended to mid-river.

For several years the two states hurled claims and counterclaims across the stream. But in 1811, the year Stevens launched the *Juliana*, the New York legis-

One of the first of the Fulton ferries. She has a double hull and an extraordinarily tall funnel. There is another ferry at the far left. The sailing craft are all gaff-rigged sloops, common enough in the early nineteenth century. Notice the burning building at the right.

lature fashioned a sharper weapon: any steam vessel other than those authorized by the monopoly could be seized and declared forfeit.

Fulton and Livingston, though first interested in the New York to Brooklyn ferry, also had plans for a New Jersey service, to run from Paulus Hook to Manhattan Island. The New York Ferry Committee, which granted a license to Stevens in 1810 on condition he provide a steam ferry within two years, granted a similar license to Fulton and Livingston for their Paulus Hook service.

The seizure act was passed after Stevens had laid up the *Juliana* for the win-

ter after her first weeks of ferrying. When spring came he decided the risk of sending her across the river was too great, even though he had built a new landing with floating stairs on the New York side near Washington Market. He kept the *Juliana* idle in Hoboken for a time, then decided that, like the *Phoenix*, she should be sent to more hospitable waters. So one day she steamed away from Hoboken toward the Connecticut River. Her course, inevitably, was around Manhattan and up Long Island Sound; she was sighted, and six boatloads of men put out from shore to stop her. But, paddle wheels chunking furiously, and under a great cloud of black smoke, she outran them and arrived safely at Middletown, far up the Connecticut.

Stevens was now out of the New York steam ferry race. He substituted team-boats rather than fight the monopoly. Fulton and William Cutting put their first

HARPER'S WEEKLY, NOVEMBER 2, 1872

A ticket for the Fulton Ferry crossing the East River from Brook-lyn to Manhattan. The price is four cents, hardly different from the present nickel fare for the much longer trip from Manhattan to Staten Island. Notice the crude, twin-hull shape of the ferry.

steam ferryboat, the *Nassau*, in service from Brooklyn in 1814. The next year Fulton died, and his successors floundered badly for a time. They tried to escape a commitment to provide a second steam ferry; a few years later they were in trouble with the ferry committee. It was charged that they had increased rates without lawful authority; that they often hired out the steamboat for other pur-poses, taking her off the ferry run; that they failed to keep the ferry clean and in repair; that even in good weather there were often long delays in service; and that "the new directors evinced an overbearing spirit little calculated to remove real grounds of complaint."

Now a new figure entered the situation: Cornelius Vanderbilt. As a young man in 1810 living on his parents' Staten Island farm, he told his mother he wanted to go sea. She agreed that if he would first plow and plant a tract of ground, she would lend him enough to buy a periauger. A short time later he had his boat and was learning the semi-piratical business of ferrying between Stapleton on Staten Island and Whitehall Landing at Manhattan's southern tip. The piratical aspects were unregulated competition, some operators with licenses, some without, all scrambling for customers, snatching them away from each other's landings, and cutting rates.

Vanderbilt did well, repaying his mother within a year, and by 1815 he could boast that he had the fastest periaugers afloat. He had seen the steam ferries on

HARPER'S WEEKLY, NOVEMBER 2, 1872

Peter Coffee, pilot of the *Nassau*, one of the Fulton Ferry boats.

the Brooklyn run, the *Nassau, Long Island Star,* and *Decatur,* but in a half-way decent breeze he could out-run any of them. Publicly, at least, he refused to take steamboats seriously. But in 1817 Daniel Tompkins, a former New York governor, began operating the steamboat *Nautilus* as a ferry from Staten Island. Vanderbilt sized up the situation and withdrew, and shortly went to work for Thomas Gibbons, operator of a steam ferry between New York and New Jersey.

View of Hoboken taken from the Ferry.

THE EDWARD W. C. ARNOLD COLLECTION, METROPOLITAN MUSEUM OF ART;
PHOTOGRAPH COURTESY MUSEUM OF THE CITY OF NEW YORK

Hoboken, New Jersey, 1838. The steam ferry *Hoboken* has just departed the landing at Hoboken, en route to Manhattan. The ferry is small and crude, without protection from storm or sun. The Jersey shore is still rural and pleasanter than it would ever be afterwards.

Gibbons had been a partner of Aaron Ogden in operating a steam ferry from Elizabethport to Manhattan, duly licensed by the Fulton-Livingston interests. But Gibbons had broken with Ogden and obtained a coasting license from the federal government, on the strength of which he began operating a rival steam ferry on the same route.

New York authorities hesitated to invoke their seizure law, because New Jersey had countered with an equally punitive measure, that anyone whose boat was seized by New York could capture and hold in retaliation any boat owned by any New York citizen! In another remarkable law the New Jersey legislators decreed that if a New Jersey citizen should be enjoined or restrained by writ or order of a New York court, the plaintiffs would be liable to the aggrieved for all damages and triple costs.

Clearly the powers of the federal government were about to meet a severe test. Georgia, Massachusetts, Pennsylvania, Tennessee, New Hampshire, Vermont, and the Territory of Orleans had made grants similar to the one New York gave Livingston. Retaliatory acts, like those of New Jersey, were equally numerous. Connecticut, for one, flatly forbade any vessel licensed by the Fulton-Livingston group to enter her waters.

With such support from his state's government, Stevens decided that he could finally risk open defiance of the monopoly. In May 1822 he put in service a new steam ferry, the *Hoboken*, with the approval of the New York Ferry Committee, which did not take sides with the State. The New York *Evening Post* described the vessel as "the beautiful steam ferryboat . . . which unites all that is desirable in speed, convenience, safety and economy." She was 98 feet long, had a 26-foot beam, was listed as being 200 tons, and steamed at 9 miles per hour.

The New York and New Jersey Steamboat Company filed an action against Stevens, but he was not backing down now. He soon added a second steam double-ender, the *Pioneer*, to his Hoboken Ferry. She ran to Canal Street, and for her time, was a ferry of unusual luxury. Not only was she larger and faster than the *Hoboken*, but she was fitted with a ladies' cabin, which was carpeted, heated, and provided with mirrors.

While Stevens was sued and enjoined, these cases were never settled decisively. The case that made history had as its formal antagonists the former partners, Ogden and Gibbons, but behind them were arrayed substantial forces: for Ogden, the Fulton-Livingston interests and the State of New York; for Gibbons, Cornelius Vanderbilt, Stevens, other independent operators, and the State of New Jersey.

Ogden opened the battle, obtaining from New York an injunction requiring that Gibbons cease his ferrying operations. Gibbons refused, and Cornelius Vanderbilt as captain of the ferry *Mouse-in-the-Mountain* was, for a time, a fugitive

NEW YORK PUBLIC LIBRARY, PHELPS STOKES COLLECTION

Hoboken, 1856. The city has grown tremendously since 1838, though in this view it is still a much handsomer town than present-day Hoboken. There is a large, formal ferry terminal, served by horse-drawn railway cars. Four steam ferries are shown. One is partially screened by smoke in the center slip, two others are just entering or departing, and the fourth, the *John Fitch,* is well clear. Notice how the slips and the ferries themselves have taken on essentially the same appearance they have today. The big sailing vessels are for ocean or coastwise trading.

from justice, continuing to operate the ferry while New York police were attempting to arrest him.

Gibbons quickly took advantage of New Jersey's retaliatory laws, bringing suit against Ogden. Though Ogden was a former state governor, a New Jersey court awarded Gibbons a full judgment, damages and triple costs.

But this left the New York injunction still in force, and Gibbons appealed to the Supreme Court of the United States. Vanderbilt was responsible for retaining as their counsel Daniel Webster, the best-known attorney in the land at the time. It was the first case to be brought before the Court under the commerce clause of the Constitution, and Chief Justice John Marshall, who handed down the decision on March 2, 1824, met the issues broadly and squarely:

What is commerce? Commerce is intercourse. What commerce is interstate? Commerce between two or more states, but not stopping at the state boundary. What authority may the states exercise over interstate commerce when the Federal Congress has acted with respect to the same subject matter? If there is any conflict, the law of Congress prevails.

Thus the Fulton-Livingston monopoly was declared unconstitutional and was broken, releasing a flood of new capital anxious to pour into the steamboat industry. The day of the teamboat was over in eastern waters. Within a decade new steam ferry lines had been established at Albany and at Newburgh on the Hudson, at Norfolk, Virginia, and at Boston and New Bedford, Massachusetts.

Today every law student is expected to become familiar with the case of Gibbons vs. Ogden, for this case, which began with a ferryboat, led to the first, and a lasting, definition of federal powers to regulate commerce and navigation.

Tales of Two Cities: Detroit and Chicago

CHAPTER TEN

MOST AMERICAN CITIES are situated beside water, be it a river, a lake or a bay. This was as true of Indian camps and settlements as of our own communities, for not only do all people need a convenient water supply but also, before roads were built, water transportation was the easiest and most convenient method of travel. Later the waterside settlements became the intersections of land and water routes. White men have added another need for watercourses: as carriers of waste; with growing populations most American rivers have become open sewers, carrying more tonnage of waste and topsoil than all man-made vehicles combined.

The major seaboard cities were ports; most of the inland cities were strategic traffic points. While the principal settlement might grow up on one side of the stream, it was usually complemented by a smaller town on the other. So there was daily traffic across the water between them, local residents on business and travelers coming through. Thus San Francisco has its Oakland; Kansas City, Missouri its Kansas City, Kansas; the westbound traveler reaches St. Louis, Missouri, through East St. Louis, Illinois; and Minneapolis and St. Paul are partners. A few cities, such as Pittsburgh, have swallowed up earlier towns on both sides of the stream.

Cross-stream traffic was heaviest, of course, at these urban places, and here the pressure was greatest to substitute bridges for ferries. The first bridge over the Charles River at Boston was built in 1786. Ten years later a floating bridge was thrown across the Schuylkill near Philadelphia. The Connecticut was bridged at Hartford in 1809. Zane's Ferry across the Muskingum was replaced by a bridge before 1819.

About 1800 an enterprising gentleman proposed that a bridge be built across the East River from New York to Brooklyn. He said he could do it in two years, but no one took him seriously. A good prophet, he was a poor engineer, for in 1800

89

A Currier & Ives visualization of the Brooklyn Bridge, published in 1872, eleven years before the completion of the great span. Notice the ferryboat in the center, doomed by the bridge, and the big Sound steamer further out in the stream.

the materials necessary for a long crossing of deep water were not at hand. Even when the Roeblings undertook to do it, there were doubts that they could succeed, and the Brooklyn Bridge, which they opened to traffic in 1883, was a tremendous step beyond any bridges built before then.

The success of the Roeblings' suspension bridge opened a new day in bridge-building, and crossings which had once seemed impossible were now brought at least within the scope of imagination. Even so, the George Washington Bridge, the San Francisco Bay Bridge, and the Chesapeake Bay Bridge were far in the future, not only for engineering reasons but also because of the volume of traffic necessary to support their great cost. Consequently not until 1941 were all the Detroit ferries, for example, to be replaced by steel bridges and tunnels.

The story of the Detroit ferries, a more peaceful one than New York's, began with a treaty with England in 1796, which was followed by a wave of immigration through Canada. On February 1, 1798, Winthrop Sargent, our old friend of the Northwest Territory, granted to John Askin the first ferry license to carry passengers for hire across the Detroit River. By 1802 traffic was heavy enough to call for more specific regulation of ferries, and the Court of General Quarter Sessions issued licenses to Askin and Gabriel Godfroy. The approved rate of ferriage was a shilling for a man, and three shillings for a horse, except in winter, when it was one shilling sixpence and four shillings.

Other licenses were issued in 1803 and in 1804. In 1820 the Court laid down rules for improved performance: "Each ferry shall be provided with two sufficient and safe canoes or ferry-boats, and one like sufficient safe scow or flat. From the first day of April until the first of November in each year, each ferry shall be attended by two good and faithful men, and from the first day of November to the first of April by three like good and faithful hands. The ferry shall be kept open from the rising of the sun until ten o'clock at night, and at all time, when practicable, shall transport the mail or other public express."

Sailing vessels were used as ferries when heavier cargo was to be transported. Then in 1825, at about the time the last teamboat was retired in New York waters, the first one appeared on the Detroit River. "The Boat is so constructed that wagons and carriages can be driven on it with ease and safety," ferrymen D. C. McKinstry and John Burtis advertised. Built in Cleveland, this teamboat made the long trip (for a ferry) to Detroit on its own horse-power.

Detroiters were, in fact, acquainted with steamboats before the team ferry arrived. Seven years earlier, in 1818, the first steam vessel on Lake Erie, *Walk-in-the-Water*, had made a spectacular trip to Detroit from Buffalo. The voyage usually took two weeks by sailboat; the *Walk-in-the-Water* left Buffalo on August 23rd and arrived in Detroit only four days later.

The *Argo,* first steamboat built in the Detroit area. Unsuccessful as a river steamer, she became a ferry, the first steam ferry on the Detroit River.

Half a dozen other lake steamers were already operating by 1827, when John Burtis, the teamboat operator, launched the *Argo,* the first steam vessel to be built in Detroit. She was hardly an impressive beginning. Her hull was two hollowed logs, planked over. Her engine, so it was claimed, could deliver four horsepower, enough to drive her at two miles an hour. Burtis used her for service to Port Huron, sixty miles away, but she proved to be so cranky to handle and such a glutton for fuel that several stops had to be made along the way. A frequent passenger was Thomas Palmer, a man of not inconsequential girth. When Palmer came aboard, the *Argo's* master hastily placed a stout chair amidship and urged Palmer to be seated. For when that heavy gentleman strode to the rail on either side, the opposite paddlewheel was lifted out of the water, and the *Argo* moved in sluggish circles until equilibrium was restored.

The *Argo* was soon taken off the river run and put to work as the first steam ferry on the Detroit River, shuttling between Detroit and Windsor. But the teamboat was kept active, too, until new and larger steam ferries were built. The first of these was the *Lady of the Lake* in 1834 and the second was the *United* in 1836. It was one of these, probably the *United,* that inspired a Mrs. Jameson to pen this description:

"A pretty little steamer, gayly painted, with streamers flying, and shaded by an awning, is continually passing and repassing from shore to shore. I have some-times sat in this ferryboat for a couple of hours together, pleased to remain still, and enjoy, without exertion, the cool air, the sparkling, redundant waters, and green islands;—amused meantime by the variety and conversation of the passen-gers. English immigrants and French Canadians, brisk Americans, dark, sad-look-ing Indians, folded in their blankets, farmers, storekeepers, speculators in wheat, artisans, trim girls with black eyes and short petticoats, speaking a Norman patois, and bringing baskets of fruit to the Detroit market, and over-dressed, long-waisted damsels of the city, attended by their beaux, going to make merry on the opposite shore."

More steam ferries were added, year after year. The *Alliance* came, followed by a second *Argo*, *Ariel*, *Essex* (first steel-hulled ferry in the area), *La Salle*, *Cadillac*, *Halcyon*, *Wayne*, *Pontiac*, *Columbia*, and *Ste. Claire*. The peak came after World War I. But soon the decline began, when the Ambassador Bridge and the Windsor Tunnel were opened in 1929.

The last Detroit ferry, *Halcyon*, was finally retired in 1941. She, the *La Salle*, and the *Cadillac* were then taken over by the Coast Guard for conversion to ice-breakers. The *Essex*, which had been withdrawn from ferry service ten years ear-lier, had become a tugboat. The *Pontiac* was being remodeled as a showboat, but before the job was finished she burned at her pier. The *Wayne*, after five years of idleness, broke from her moorings and drifted out into the channel one day for a last, lonely cruise. But a fireboat caught her, and soon after she was broken up. The *Columbia* and *Ste. Claire* had a more dignified final fling; in May, 1939, they were put back in service for a day to carry passengers who wished to see King George and Queen Elizabeth on their royal visit to Windsor. Then they, too, went on the scrap heap.

Mark Beaubien of Detroit was twenty-six when he decided to seek his fortune farther west. He wrote later of his migration: "I arrived in Chicago in the year of 1826, from Detroit; came with my family by team; no road only Indian trail. I had to hire an Indian to show me the way to Chicago. I camped out doors and bought a log house from Jim Kinzie. There was no town laid out; didn't expect no town. When they laid out the town, my house laid out in the street; when they laid the town I bought two lots where I built the old Sauganash, the first frame house in Chicago."

Our picture shows why Chicago, as it became a town, needed ferries. The Chicago River, with its two branches, curves around the center of the city, em-bracing a section not much larger than the present Loop. Only from the south can the city be reached without crossing the river.

The first ferry in Chicago served Fort Dearborn, but at the time this was not operated primarily for the convenience of the traveling public. No doubt there were casual ferries in earlier years, but the first recognized ferry operator was Beaubien, who was licensed by the Cook County Commissioners in 1831. All local residents were to be carried free; strangers were to pay fixed rates.

Beaubien bought a flatboat for sixty-five dollars and worked at ferrying in a desultory way. It was hardly an important commercial venture. Customers were not numerous, and the river was so narrow that it took but a moment or two to set them across. Beaubien had other interests, and the ferry was often left unattended, passengers ferrying themselves across. Beaubien was later ordered to have a ferryman on duty each day from dawn to dusk.

With so little interest in ferrying, he was undisturbed when a bridge of floating logs was thrown across the river at Randolph Street. Indeed, he was among the citizens who, a few years later, petitioned the Commissioners to build a drawbridge at Lake Street.

That was the problem: a drawbridge. For while the Chicago River was narrow, and wider streams had been bridged back east, the Chicago was a waterway on which commerce was developing rapidly. It would be impractical to build a bridge so high it would clear the tall masts of schooners, but, on the other hand, the channel must not be blocked. So there could be no bridge, except one that could be opened readily and often.

In 1834 a crude gallows bridge was built at Dearborn Street, a structure which did little to enhance the reputations of either its designer or the carpenters who pieced it together. While Chicagoans have a broad sense of humor, the joke eventually wore thin. Sailing vessels could scarcely maneuver through the narrow draw, and often they slammed into the structure. The lift frequently jammed, at times so badly that neither boats nor pedestrians could pass. Once it became stuck at the top and so remained for two full days. At last the Council ordered its removal, and a gladdened citizenry, not wanting to give the Council time to change its collective mind, descended upon it with their axes and quickly hacked it to splinters.

There were ferries at Clark and at State streets now, and the business was active and rewarding. The State Street Ferry, transferred to Dearborn when the bridge was torn down, was a scow, large enough for two teams, pulled from side to side by means of a rope passed over a windlass. There was a man to work the windlass, but impatient passengers often shoved him aside to get the job done more quickly.

Even the rope was a problem, of course, because the channel had to be cleared whenever a boat came along. The Chicago *Democrat* explained how this was done:

"He works his ferry with as much ease and assurance as the captain of one of the largest crafts upon the lake his floating palace; and we can assure our readers the task is not without its difficulties, and withal not unaccompanied by

Chicago, 1820. Notice how approaching from almost any direction, one must cross water. Though the Chicago River is narrow, it was not successfully bridged for some time, since it was used by sailing vessels with tall masts. Fort Dearborn is shown on the left bank.

danger, if not to life and limb, at least to the reputation of the ferryman. Sometimes the wind blowing strong up the creek, a brig comes bowling along with the
foresail, topgallant and jib set. An impatient citizen is on the South side with
visions of roast beef and dessert to match in his mind's eye and hunger knocking
at the walls of his stomach. Bill sees the brig. The captain halloos, 'Let go your
d——d rope!' The citizen cries, 'Come over, you have time enough.' But Bill
thinks, 'It's better to be sure of the line; if that breaks the gentleman loses his
dinner, and I may lose my place.' So he very properly lets go all, and the impatient
citizen has to wait just two minutes and a half, at which he grumbles some."

Chicago, 1834. This rope ferry crossed
the Chicago River at Fort Dearborn.
Though ferries once crossed the river
at most of the points where bridges
have since been built, this is the only
illustration of a Chicago ferry known
to the Chicago Historical Society.

Between the Clark and State street ferries there was built up considerable rivalry, citizens joining in the exchange of banter and insults much more vehemently than the ferrymen. A Clark Street enthusiast once declared war, marched to State Street with a large knife, slashed the ferry rope, and retired with the honors of battle.

A more bitter rivalry engaged the commercial interests of Chicago's North and South sides for the advantage in trading with the prairie schooners that were now arriving in large numbers. Sometimes as many as 500 gathered on the plains outside the city. As long as there was no bridge to the North side, the South-side

merchants had the advantage. So they did what they could to block construction of a bridge at Clark Street.

Nevertheless, the bridge was built, and in the next few years others were built, too. However, bridge-building failed to keep pace with the city's growth, so there was still business for the ferrymen, though Chicago citizens demanded that all ferries now be made free.

Then came the winter of 1849, with a fearful flood and then an ice jam. Every bridge in the city was carried away, and vast damage was done to the hundreds of sailing vessels moored along the river banks. For a few months the ferries again had a monopoly. But not for long. Ferries could not, over so narrow a river, offer such service as a bridge, and the latter were soon rebuilt. Shortly, indeed, there were many new bridges, at Madison, Clark, Wells, Kinzie, Van Buren, and Lake streets.

But the ferries were not finished yet, for Chicago grew at a tremendous rate, and the bridges were often jammed with traffic. Even as late as 1856 ferries were still still operating at Randolph, Wells and Chicago Streets, and at Lake House.

About the last chapter was a tragedy at the Lake House ferry. It happened on the morning of September 19, 1856. The regular ferry was out of service, needing repairs, and an old flat scow had been borrowed from Wells Street. Thus service was slower than usual, and a great crowd of impatient commuters gathered on the north bank. As the ferry returned from a crossing, they surged aboard. The ferryman protested, but they pushed him ashore and set forth without him. The scow, loaded far beyond its reasonable capacity, lurched out to midstream and capsized. Some passengers swam the short distance to shore. Some were picked up by boats. Ten bodies were found, but the number of dead was never definitely fixed.

West to the Mississippi

~~~~~~

Chapter Eleven

Maps tell the story of how America was discovered, explored and settled. Two maps, one of them printed here in two sections, record the progress of 120 years. The older of these was photographed from Speed's *Atlas*, a monumental work published in England in 1676. By then numerous parties of explorers had sailed down the New England coastline and beyond, giving names to the capes and headlands and islands. There were settlements at Boston, New Plymouth, and a few other places along the coastline, and on the shores of the principal rivers. But much of the land was as yet unknown, or known only by rumor and inaccurate reports of exploring parties.

No one, for example, had traveled by the route shown on this map up the Merrimac River to the Lake of the Iroquois; there is no such route, nor any such lake as shown here. The Iroquois were not kindly disposed toward visitors, and their country was known only by legend.

By comparing this map with a modern one, you can make many deductions about the times and the kind of source materials available to this map-maker, especially if you read along with it such a fine summary of early investigations as *The Explorers of North America* by John Bartlet Brebner.* On the Speed map Rhode Island *is* an island, in Narragansett Bay. Nantucket, Martha's Vineyard and the Elizabeth Islands are shown in roughly the proper locations, but their relative sizes are all wrong. The cartographer's information about the Hudson River was fairly good up to the Mohawk, which Henry Hudson first reached in 1609, but beyond that it failed. There is no indication here of Lake Champlain. But if you will locate Lake St. Peter on a modern map, between Montreal and

* Doubleday & Company, 1955.

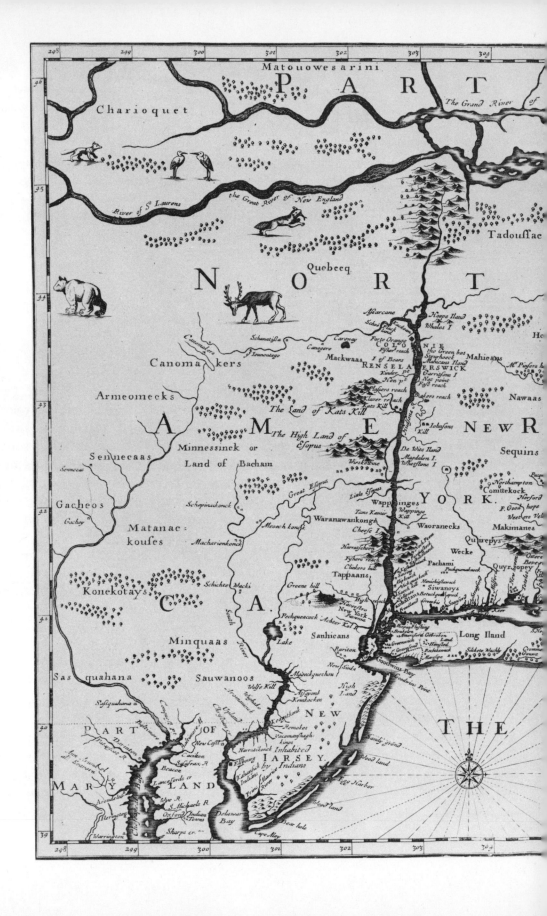

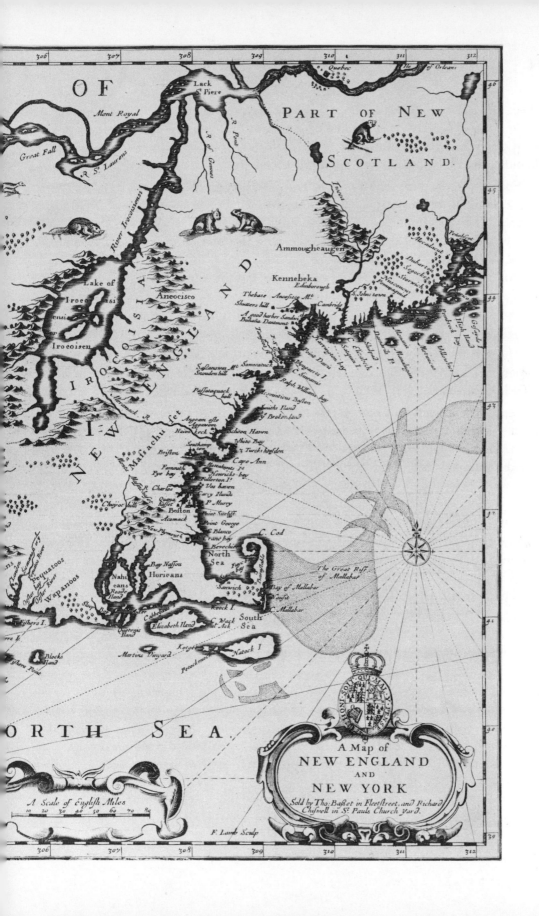

A Map of
NEW ENGLAND
AND
NEW YORK

Sold by Tho: Baßet in Fleetstreet, and Richard
Chiswell in St Pauls Church yard.

A Scale of English Miles

F. Lamb Sculp.

Quebec, and relate it to "Lack St. Piere" on the Speed map, much becomes clear. Speed's Lake of the Iroquois is Lake Champlain, first seen by white men who came from the north, by way of the St. Lawrence. The relationship between northern and southern entries was as yet not understood.

No ferry routes are shown on this map, but, as we know, there were ferries in service even then: at Boston; on the Connecticut River; on both sides of Manhattan Island; at New Castle on the Delaware; and other places as well. By then a number of ferries were operating in Virginia. But the ferries were not yet "floating sections of highway." The roads were yet to come. White men, except for those who explored or traded for furs, clung to the water's edge.

The second map, in two sections, is Abraham Bradley, Jr.'s. Published in 1796, it is one of the earliest American road maps. This is far better than Speed's map. Its outlines, boundaries and place locations are based on quite precise data. Even though its showing of mountains is conventionalized rather than definitive, and there are numerous improvisations in defining the paths of lesser rivers to the west, it is a remarkable job of showing where, in those days, men lived and traveled.

People sometimes think of a frontier as a rim of civilization, a more or less regular perimeter pushed slowly westward. But it was not like that. First came the explorers—and this term has been used to include many different kinds of people who dared the wilderness for quite different reasons. Some sought knowledge and shared what they found. Others were seeking gold or furs or souls to save. Whatever their purpose, they were not trained observers, and frequently their reports were a blend of faulty recollection and misinformation gathered from Indians.

The Spaniards came primarily in search of gold. They seized what gold and valuables they found, destroyed the cities and towns, slew their inhabitants, and left ruin behind them. Furs attracted the French *coureurs de bois* down the St. Lawrence, up the Ottawa, and on long, bold journeys west and south of Lake Michigan, but few Frenchmen followed behind them to settle the land. Dutch and Swedes and others came, but it was the English colonists who took the firmest grasp on the new continent and began to build on its soil.

The Bradley map reveals what happened then and much of how it happened. To make the map more readable when reproduced here, I arranged to have the roads retouched, outlining them boldly. Imagine now how this map would look if each road were to be extended as a shaded band ten to twenty miles wide, and if similar shaded areas were placed over the settled coastlines and watercourses. This would be a roughly accurate way of defining the land area then known, settled, traveled, and otherwise used.

The shaded area would cover much of the land in the New England states, excluding Maine and the mountainous parts of New Hampshire and Vermont. A broad band of heavily-shaded area would extend from southern New York down the coast to Georgia.

If one looks a little to the west of the densest sections, one can see how this pattern developed. In western New York State, men traveled along the rivers and settled. Then came paths and roads connecting the rivers, and in time other settlements were established along these roads.

Look at the pattern then developing along the southern rivers, those flowing into the Gulf of Mexico. Much of this land area is innocent of roads; there are many Indian villages, some forts and trading posts, a few settlements. On the Mississippi, settlement had extended up from New Orleans to Natchez.

Much of the inland route connecting the northeastern cities and the Gulf was provided by nature: the more than 2,500-mile system of the Mississippi and the Ohio. The missing link lay between the Ohio and the Susquehanna, a mere 150 miles overland through Pennsylvania. Once it was possible to haul cargo by wagon across the mountain passes, the heartland of America was open to development.

The map shows how this was done: crossing the Susquehanna at Harris' Ferry, then westward, through towns now located along the route. The traveler could stop for refreshment at Carlisle or Shippensburg, at Bedford before crossing the mountains, then at Wells Tavern, and on through Greensburg to Pittsburgh and the Ohio River. With this link completed, the Ohio River became a much-traveled waterway, settlers loading their belongings on rafts and flatboats to float downstream to a place of their choice.

Now look again at the more heavily settled portions of the country, and the Bradley map shows another stage of development. Roads now *parallel* the original water routes. The post road links Boston and New York. A road runs beside the Hudson all the way to Albany, another beside the Connecticut for much of its length. Tracing this pattern west, still another aspect of it appears: roads cutting across country where the water route is circuitous. There is, for example, a road from Pittsburgh to Wheeling. No doubt the downstream journey was easier than the land route, but the return trip was quicker and easier by road.

Where were the ferries? The map gives ample evidence of how essential they were to the country's development. Narrow streams and creeks were sometimes bridged; shallow rivers could be forded; in winter many streams were crossed on the ice. But for the most part, where Bradley's map shows a road crossing a river of any consequence, there was a ferry.

With a little patience and frequent references to a modern map, it is a fascinating game to trace on this old Bradley map the routes of early American travelers, many of whom compiled lengthy journals during their wanderings.

Andre Michaux was a French botanist who came to America in 1785 to study forest trees. He lived in New York for a year or so, then moved to Charleston where

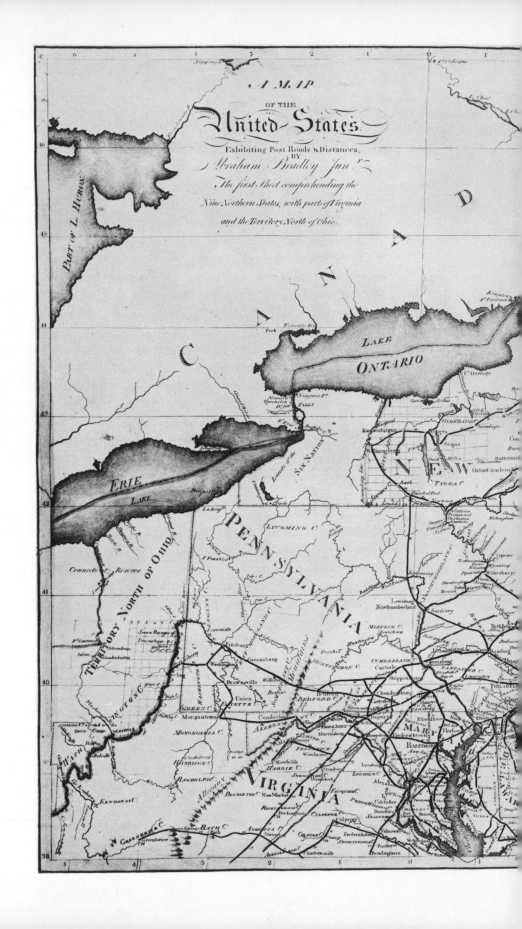

A MAP OF THE United-States. Exhibiting Post Roads & Distances, BY Abraham Bradley Jun. The first Sheet comprehending the Nine Northern States, with parts of Virginia and the Territory North of Ohio.

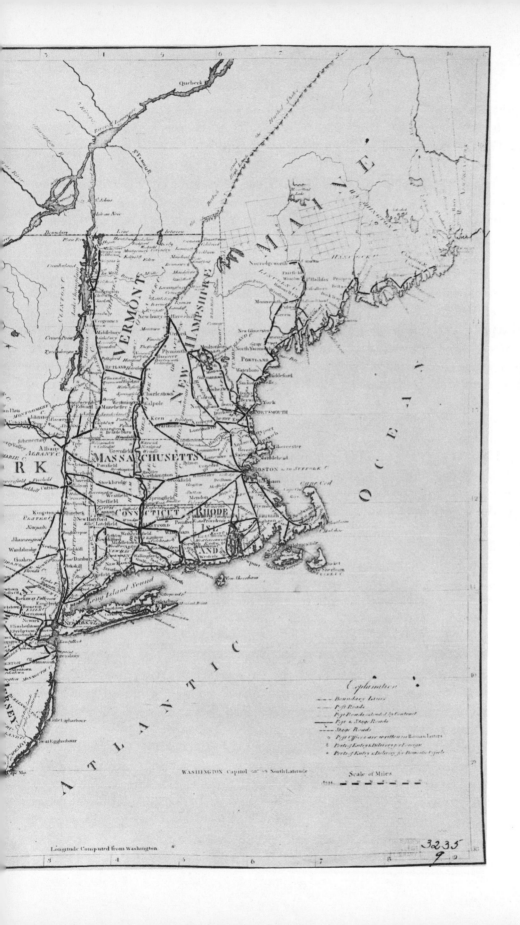

he bought a plantation. From there he set out on many expeditions, ranging from Canada to the Bahamas, noting plant life, people, and occasionally, the ferries.

In 1793 he was returning from a trip to Kentucky, bound for Philadelphia. He came through the Cumberland Gap by the route shown on the map which passed through the letter "C" in the state named "KENTUCKY." He ferried across the Clinch River, and took the road running northeast through Abingdon, Virginia, and Wythe Court House. His journal says he crossed the New River on "Peper's Ferry." This must have been by an alternate route not shown on this map, for Pepper's Ferry was upstream from the Ingles Ferry, shown on this map as "English's Ferry." Then he was on the road again, up the Shenandoah Valley through Lexington, Staunton, Woodstock, and Winchester. On December sixth he "passed by Harspur (Harper's) Ferry across the Potomack and entered Maryland."

Harper's Ferry isn't shown on Bradley's map. It is at the confluence of the Shenandoah and Potomac rivers, near the location of "Sheperdsto." where James Rumsey, a few years earlier, had demonstrated his steamboat.

The road Michaux traveled from Harper's Ferry to Harrisburg wasn't shown on Bradley's original map. But it, or something like it, appears in the illustration, because some kind visitor to the library where I found the map had added it in rough pencil marks.

In 1795 Michaux was off again, leaving Charleston for Kentucky, and the game becomes more interesting now, because this was a date close to that of publication of Bradley's map. So we find this entry in Michaux's journal: "Wednesday, 20th of May, passed by Green Court house 27 Miles from John's Borough and the road to Kentuckey, taking the right hand and passing by the ferry on the Holston River."

According to Bradley, it was Greenville, 20 miles from Jonesboro, Tennessee, and the Holstein River. On the other hand, Bradley doesn't show the road by which Michaux "arrived at Colonel King's on the Houlston River at the place called Macby ferry 15 miles from Iron Works," or the road beyond McBee's Ferry whereby Michaux came to Knoxville.

This was not necessarily a defect in Bradley's work. He showed, with remarkable accuracy, the better-used routes of the day, primarily those used by stages and carriers of the mail. He did not attempt to show every trail and trace, any more than a modern road map shows unmaintained dirt tracks which cross rural and forest lands today.

The ferrymen along these routes were men of substance. The ferry controlled the river crossing, and it attracted trade and gossip. Ferrymen were usually engaged in other activities as well, tavern-keeping, farming, trading.

Michael Simpson of the Paxtang went off to fight in the Revolutionary War, and by his conduct rose to the rank of General. After the war he bought a house and ferry on the Susquehanna. George Washington slept there when he visited his former colleague at the time of the Whisky Rebellion.

Another who turned from soldiering to ferrying was Colonel Nicholas Raoul. He commanded Napoleon's advance guard on the march from Elba to Paris in 1815. After Napoleon's crushing defeat at Waterloo, a number of Frenchmen, Raoul among them, came to America and settled Demopolis in western Alabama. Raoul's land was on the Tombigbee River (the "Tumbeckbe" according to Bradley), and he established a ferry there.

A third ex-soldier was Major Robert Benham. By 1800 many travelers had made the water journey all the way from Pittsburgh to New Orleans. While it seems, in modern times, an odd decision, a military expedition of about a hundred men, Benham among them, was once sent all the way from the upper Ohio to New Orleans, to bring back arms for outposts on the northern borders of Virginia.

On their return trip, they had just passed the settlement at Cincinnati when they sighted Indians, in rafts and canoes, emerging from the mouth of the Little Miami River, crossing to a point of land on the southern shore of the Ohio.

Colonel Rogers, in command, gave orders to land and attack. But he had misjudged the strength of the Indian party and the quality of their weapons. He and his men were overwhelmed, all but a few killed or captured. Major Benham lay shot through both hips, unable to move. He was convinced all of his comrades were dead.

On the second day, Benham saw a raccoon approaching. Famished and desperate, he decided that if the coon came close enough he'd risk firing a shot, even though it might be heard by the Indians if they were still nearby. He shot the coon, and a moment later was cautiously hailed by another survivor, who had also thought himself alone.

By coincidence, it happened that this poor fellow had been wounded in both arms, so badly he could move neither, but he had full use of his legs. With a full set of limbs between them, Benham and his comrade managed to survive in the woods for six weeks while their wounds healed.

Benham went back to Cincinnati and settled there. This was the same Robert Benham who, on February 18, 1792, obtained from Winthrop Sargent, Secretary of the Northwest Territory, the first license to operate a ferry from Cincinnati across the Ohio.

The opening of the central portion of America was not just a matter of exploring, improving trails into roads, and providing ferries across the streams. For a time the water route from Quebec to New Orleans was a French lifeline on the continent. When the European peace treaties of 1763 put an end to French power in America, the Ottawa chief, Pontiac, built a tribal alliance that effectively blocked the route to English colonists from the east. At the same time other Indian groups

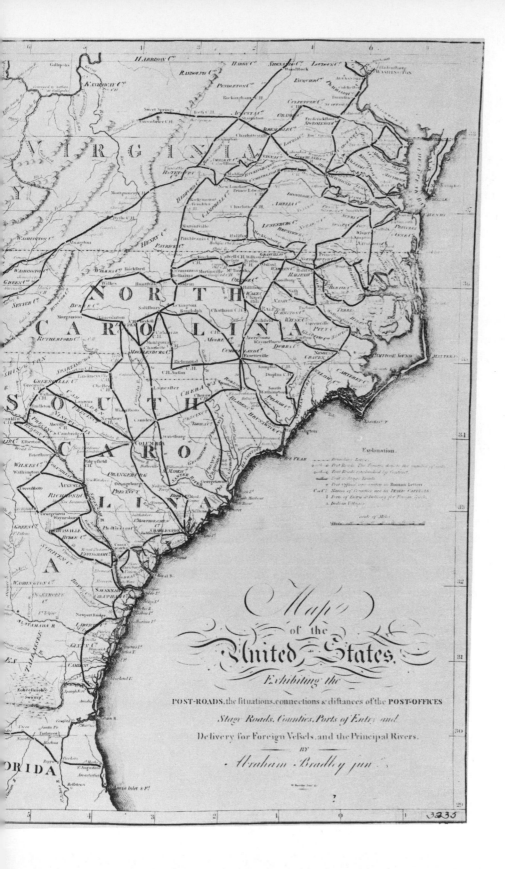

Map
of the
United States,
Exhibiting the
POST-ROADS, the situations, connections & distances of the POST-OFFICES
Stage Roads, Counties, Ports of Entry and
Delivery for Foreign Vessels, and the Principal Rivers.
BY
Abraham Bradley jun.

were now defending their lands and hunting-grounds against white invaders. One grievance of the colonists against the British government was its attempt to keep them from moving westward. Only after the Revolution did the land-seekers begin large-scale movements inland, driving the Indians before them, slaughtering those who resisted.

Comparing the Speed and Bradley maps indicates how far displacement of the Indians had gone in 120 years. By the close of the 18th century no Indian strongholds remained in the thirteen original colonies. In the south, Indian resistance continued, but in many cases it succeeded only because white men had not yet hungered for those particular lands. It was the white man's country now, west to the Mississippi.

But the Missouri had not yet been explored. In 1792 Thomas Jefferson, President Washington's Secretary of State, had proposed that Andre Michaux be sent on an expedition to seek the rumored link between the Missouri and Columbia rivers, but Michaux had been recalled to France before this could be done. When Jefferson became President, and following the Louisiana Purchase of 1803, he sent Captain Meriwether Lewis and William Clark on this same quest. Since before Columbus' time, the geographies of North America had been compounded of fable and supposition. Men had come in search of Cathay, of a northwest passage, or of other water routes to the Pacific. Now the last of the legends was laid to rest.

The land was big, but now the area east of the Mississippi was being tamed and settled. Newcomers were arriving in greater and greater numbers, from the north, crossing at John Askin's ferry over the Detroit River; from the east, setting out from Wright's or Harris' ferries over the Susquehanna en route to Pittsburgh on the Ohio; by the southern route along the Cumberland Road; up the Mississippi from New Orleans, joining with those who spread downstream from the Ohio.

Almost everywhere, ferrymen were among the first settlers, or, to put it more accurately, a first settler was very likely to take up ferrying. Ownership of land where road met river carried with it, in most jurisdictions, the right of ferriage, and this right became increasingly valuable as more and more people used the roads.

The Mississippi River was the most formidable water crossing ferrymen had yet attempted. Crossing from shore to shore was trickier than floating downstream or hauling a keelboat upstream along the banks. But soon after the turn of the century, ferries were put in service at some points along the Mississippi, and along the Missouri, too.

Eli Langford's ferry was on the Mississippi, thirty miles below the mouth of the Illinois. On April 3, 1810, Thomas Weeks, a settler, and his family arrived at the ferry, planning to spend the night and cross early next morning.

James Beeman, who lived nearby, helped them load the ferry that evening in preparation for an early start. But next morning they found the ferry and their goods gone. Beeman then remembered having seen a group of Pottawatomie Indians upstream the day before; going to investigate, Weeks and Beeman found they had vanished.

Two weeks later this same group of Indians, led by a local chief named Main Pock, was seen in Peoria, and news of this reached Weeks. In Peoria, Antoine Robidoux said he had seen the Indians wearing white men's clothing, and thought it remarkable at the time. The blacksmith said he had noticed household tools in their possession, but Main Pock had told him they found the gear in a canoe lying abandoned on a sand bar.

This was enough evidence for Weeks and he filed a lawsuit—against the Government of the United States. He demanded "six hundred and five Dollars and fifty four cents & one eighth of a cent" as recompense for his stolen property.

Wilmington, North Carolina. This view of the central part of town was sketched from the ferry landing, probably before 1820. The flatboat ferry crossing the Cape Fear River with a covered wagon on board is propelled by oars.

How many ferries were there in America by, say, 1825? The best estimate I can make is about three hundred known, regular, established ferries, providing more or less constant service, east of the Mississippi River. That estimate is based on recorded licenses, old maps, the journals of travelers, and similar sources—and it is, if anything, too low.

Team-boats, propelled by horses, were beginning to appear at some points along the western rivers. There was one across the Ohio at Maysville. Another was near Cincinnati. This latter ferry, Anderson's, is still in business; for many years it was owned and operated by the Kottmeyer family of Constance, Kentucky. Charles Kottmeyer was the ferryman in the early 19th century and made the change from flatboats to the teamboat. Horsepower ultimately gave way to steam, and the Kottmeyer's built their own steamboat, the *Boone*, a cranky little vessel that barely managed to chug across the stream. This was the first of six Kottmeyer-built steam ferries. Not until 1937 and *Boone* Number 7 did they go to a shipyard, to purchase a steel-hulled boat.

Another team-boat at Cincinnati was operated by the Kennedy family. Their history claims they were the first ferrymen here, though other records indicate Benham preceded them by a few years. They were unusual in that they settled on both sides of the river, Thomas at the Kentucky landing, Francis on the Ohio side. Francis was drowned while ferrying cattle for Mad Anthony Wayne's army during the latter's campaign against the Indians.

The first steamboat on the western rivers was the *New Orleans*. She was built at Pittsburgh in 1811 for the Fulton-Livingston interests. Acting as their agent was the second of John Stevens' old associates, Nicholas Roosevelt!

The *New Orleans* was 140 feet long, advertised as able to carry 400 tons of cargo and to accommodate passengers in "elegant comfort." Advertising also claimed she could make 3 miles an hour upstream, against a 2½ mile an hour current, and would make the voyage from New Orleans to Pittsburgh in six weeks.

She never did it. Accounts differ as to her downstream voyage. One puts her in Louisville on November 15, 1811, and at Natchez on January 1. Another says she left Pittsburgh early in December and arrived in New Orleans the day before Christmas.

After her long voyage, the *New Orleans* was put in service between New Orleans and Natchez, making the round trip in five to seven days. On July 14, 1814, she hit a snag at Baton Rouge, damaging the hull beyond repair. Her engine and copper boiler were later installed in another *New Orleans*, which sailed the lower Mississippi for only a few months before she too struck a snag and sank.

Another river steamboat, the *Comet*, was built at Pittsburgh in 1813. After the downstream trip to New Orleans and a single round-trip to Natchez, she was sold, and her engine was taken out and installed in a cotton gin.

The same year the Fulton-Livingston interests tried again, building the *Vesuvius* at Pittsburgh. She made a successful voyage to New Orleans in 1814 and started back up the river, but on July 14—apparently an unlucky day—she ran aground. She floated free in December and returned to New Orleans, where she was commandeered for military service by General Jackson. She promptly ran aground again. Refloated, she was put in freight service between New Orleans and Natchez, but a few months later caught fire and burned to the water's edge.

The *Comet* had engines built to the design of Daniel French, who patented a steam engine in 1809. He now built a boat of his own, the *Enterprise*. It was generally believed at the time that steamboats were not practical for use above Natchez, because of their slow speed, but French's boat was relatively fast. She made the downstream trip in fourteen days, then returned to Pittsburgh, the first steamboat to make the entire ascension. The following year she sank in the Ohio.

None of these were ferries. Indeed, the first record I can find of a steam ferry on the Mississippi or Missouri is at St. Louis in 1853, though by then steamboats were relatively common and occasionally, no doubt, one was pressed into temporary service as a ferry.

A more common scene was a flatboat ferry operating across the river, while the steamboats chugged up and downstream. The flatboat was a modest investment, and it often paid handsome returns. A single man and horse would be carried for fifty cents. Another dollar or so would be earned ashore by feeding and stabling the horse, and selling its rider a meal, a pint of whisky, and a bed. From a family traveling with their household goods and livestock, the ferryman might collect better than five dollars.

As the stream of westbound migrants increased, lines backed up at many of the ferries. Some ferrymen were netting $20,000 a year! But the fabulous years were still ahead, when the lands west of the Missouri were opened to homesteaders, and when gold was discovered in California.

Ferries on the Frontier

≋≋≋≋≋≋≋≋≋≋≋≋≋≋≋≋≋≋≋≋≋≋≋≋≋≋

CHAPTER TWELVE

FREDERICK JACKSON TURNER said of the frontier that "American development has exhibited not merely advance along a single line, but a return to primitive conditions on a continually advancing frontier line, and a new development for that area. . . . In this advance, the frontier is the outer edge of the wave, the meeting point between savagery and civilization . . ."

On the frontier, the evolution of ferries, like that of so many other aspects of life, was repeated again and again. While John Stevens' steam ferry *Juliana* was hauling passengers across the Hudson on a regular schedule, John Bradbury was riding along the shore of the Missouri River with a mounted party of adventurers. Late one afternoon they came to the Knife River, and saw a village of Minitaree Indians on the other side. They hailed them.

A few of the Indians came over to parley. When a price had been agreed upon, the Indians called their ferrymen, the squaws. Six squaws came across, each in a bull-boat. They stowed the white men's gear in their boats and paddled Bradbury and his companions across, while the Indian men swam the horses over. Payment was in powder and ball.

The bull-boat was a skin canoe, fashioned by stretching untanned buffalo hide over a framework of green saplings. As the hide dried, it shrank, making a boat that was almost as light as a birchbark canoe and much less fragile, though because it was bulbous rather than slender, a paddler could not handle it as deftly.

Again repeating the eastern story, treaties were signed with Indian tribes, and a common provision was that they should provide service at the ferries along the main trails. And, as before, there were frequent complaints that the Indians were failing in this obligation or were exploiting it. Usually there were two sides to the story, though the Indians' side was seldom heard or recorded. Significantly, when Indian ferrying was criticized, there was almost always a white man ready to take over the concession the moment the Indians were displaced. And conveniently, the decisions were made in Washington, where the Indians had no voice.

An argument between two white men sometimes gave revealing glimpses of what was going on. Major William McClellan, for example, was assigned to help administer the Choctaw Treaty of 1825. For some time there had been bad blood between McClellan and Colonel Matthew Arbuckle, in command at Fort Smith, Arkansas. One issue between them concerned the ferry at Fort Smith.

A long-established Indian ferry was located here, and McClellan gave a Choctaw half-breed named Folsom permission to operate it. The Cherokees, living across the river, had some claim to the ferry rights, by custom, but Folsom was sure he could work that out with the Cherokee chiefs.

The military at Fort Smith also had a ferry, originally for their own use, and while the Indians had only small boats, the soldiers had a large flat raft. This they put in charge of two civilians, Messrs. Nick and Rogers, providing them with quarters and equipment and supplying them with food from the commissary.

Nick and Rogers, being enterprising fellows, were soon ferrying any customers who came along, and the Indian ferryman, Folsom, found his trade slipping away. Folsom approached Arbuckle with a proposition: let him have the flat, and he would ferry the military free of charge. Arbuckle turned him down. Folsom then called Nick and Rogers and served notice on them to confine their ferrying to the military, but Arbuckle broke in to declare that the military were in charge, and he would decide.

Hearing of this, Major McClellan protested formally to the Secretary of War. Arbuckle also sent a dispatch to Washington. In due course, the decision came back: McClellan was ordered to yield control of the ferry to the military commander, if the ferry landing was on military property. Of course, it was, and McClellan obeyed.

Not all of the settlers of the west came overland. New Orleans was a long-established city by now, and the Mississippi was only one of the many water highways inland from the Gulf of Mexico. Settlers had pushed up the rivers of Alabama and Mississippi and Texas. By about 1835 Groce's Ferry and Beason's ferry were doing business on the Brazos; Lewis' and Williams' ferries were on the Neches; and on the Sabine River there were at least three ferries, Patterson's, Hickman's and Gaines'.

Coming up the Mississippi and branching off to the westward on the Arkansas, pioneers settled at Little Rock, and the city was formally laid out in 1821. In 1824 the Secretary of War appointed commissioners to survey the possibilities of a road between Little Rock and a point opposite Memphis on the Mississippi.

This promised to be a difficult project, they reported, the direct route being "interspersed with lakes, Swamps &c and every where intersected with an unusual number of water courses . . ." There was a ferry, they said, just above Memphis. Another ferry would be required across Blackfish Lake, and two other lakes would have to be ferried in wet weather. The Languelle River was narrow enough to be bridged at low water, but it could be forded then; at high water only a ferry would do. They also recommended a ferry on the Cache River, another across the White.

By the end of 1826 the road was well under way. Charles Thomas, in charge of the project, reported to the Quartermaster General from his work camp in the Mississippi swamp, 14 miles inland. The need now was to attract people to operate the ferries, and this could be done, he said, by opening the lands along the route to public sale. "Expedited private persons," Thomas wrote, would buy river and lake sites and open ferries.

Ferrying was, indeed, an opportunity that attracted early settlers to many frontier areas. In 1824 the War Department asked the Indian Agent at Sulphur Fork on the Red River to take a census of the number of white families then resident. He reported that "The number of whites within the immediate vicinity of this Agency are Two families one Settled on a large Lake, for the purpose of Keeping Ferry, for the accomodation of the Indians and Travellers, and the other on a large Creek or River, for the same purpose . . ."

He added somewhat bitterly: "The Country is generally unhealthy. Subject to Bilious complaints."

Approaching the middle of the nineteenth century, the Missouri was still the frontier, but there were numbers of pioneers who crossed it and set out over the plains. In 1847 Brigham Young, leading the vanguard of Latter-Day Saints, headed west, and in due course came to the upper crossing of the North Platte River. Here he detached nine men from his party and left them with this mandate:

"Brethren as you are about to stop at this place for a little season for the purpose of passing Emagrants over the river and assisting the saints. We have thought fit to appoint Thomas Grover Superintendent of the ferry, and of your Company; which if you approve; we want you to agree that you will follow his council implicitly, and without gainsaying; and we desire that you will be agreed in all your operations, actions in Concert keeping together continually, and not scatter to hunt, &c, and at your leisure moments put up a comfortable room that will afford yourselves and your horses protection against the Indians should a war partey pass this way; but, first of all, see that your boat is propperley coupled; by fastining Raw Hides over the tops of the canoes, or some better process. Complete the Landings and be careful of the Lives and property of all you labour for, remembering that you are responsible for all accidents through your carelessness or negligence and see that ye Retain not that which belongeth to the Traveller.

"For one wagon . . . Familey &c. you will charge $1.50 for payment in Flower and Provisions at state prices; or three Dollars in cash, but you had better take young stock at a fair valuation instead of cash . . .

"Should general Emagration cease before our brethren arrive—Cachet your effects and return to Laramie and wait their arrival and come on with them to the place of location and we promise you that, the superintendent of the Ferry shall never lack wisdom or knowledge to devise and council you in righteousness and for your best good; if you will always be agreed; and in all humility watch and pray without ceasing.

"When our Emagration companies arrives: if the river is not fordable, ferry them, and let them who are able pay a reasonable sum, the council of their camp will decide who are able to pay.

A current ferry on the Platte River, probably in Nebraska. Notice the horses swimming across in the background. The ferry was solely for human beings and their equipment.

"Let a strict account be kept of every man's labour, also of all wagons and Teams &c ferried and of all receipts and expenditures, allowing each according to his labor and justice; and if any one feels aggrieved, let him not murmur; but be patient till you come up, and let the council decide and the way not to be aggrieved is for every man to Love his brother as him self."

The nine met, agreed, and signed a subscript adhering to the order. It was not long before they had a flatboat built of two dugout canoes, planked over to form a raft. For the first two years it was rowed across, one large sweep on each side, a third at the stern to serve as rudder. And they carried out their instructions to the letter, judging by the journal entries of passing travelers. A Dr. Caldwell noted: "They have but one boat here, which is a good one, & very careful hands. The Mormons appear honest so far as dealing with them. They conduct matters very well here, and have a smithery with 2 forges, but charge high. Swim the cattle, and charge $3.00 per wagon for the ferrying."

And another passer-by, William G. Johnston, wrote, "Contrary to expectation, based upon the common reputation of these Latter-Day Saints, we found those in charge of the ferry men of respectable appearance, well informed, polite, and in every way agreeable . . ."

Three dollars was a substantial price for a crossing of little more than 450 feet. But the brethren were ferried for much less. Indeed, until a current ferry was installed, the ferrymen moved the landing-place up or down-stream when Saints

THE MARINERS' MUSEUM, NEWPORT NEWS, VIRGINIA

came marching in, so their livestock could pasture on fresh, untrampled grass.

When the Gold Rush began, the Mormon ferry was on one of the principal routes to California, and the ferry became an important source of revenue for the Latter-Day Saints. By 1849 it was a current ferry, and when the rush began a new, larger boat was added to the original flat. Prices went up, too. The $3 fee was raised to $4, then to $5, and people who didn't want to risk losing their cattle in the rapid waters of the Platte could have them ferried for a dollar a head.

The Platte was bridged in 1851, but the bridge was a poor one and some distance off the best road, so the ferry kept much of its traffic. But in 1853 a big toll-bridge was built, and with its success, the Mormon ferry had ended its usefulness.

Kansas City was the principal point of departure not only for settlers but for trade with Mexico and the Southwest, California, Utah, and Oregon. In 1840 five freight companies were operating here with 60 wagons for overland hauling. By 1843 there were 30 companies with more than 350 wagons.

When the news came that gold had been found in California, the ferrying business boomed fantastically all along the western rivers. From St. Louis northward, the Mississippi ferries quickly felt the effects of the rush. Hordes of people came to the crossings at Cassville, Davenport, Burlington, Keokuk, and other

St. Louis, Missouri, 1832. The town is seen here from the Illinois side of the Mississippi. Notice the steamers in the river. The ferry, which appears to consist of a square deck over a pair of parallel hulls, has come alongside the wharf starboard (right) side to. Even though the mooring line has just been snaked over the tree stump, the passengers and cattle are almost all off. Power seems to be supplied by two horizontal boilers located just under the bridge, or porch. How the power is applied is not clear but probably through a huge center wheel located between the hulls and inside the house. This was one of the first steam ferries to cross the Mississippi at this point.

Davenport, Iowa, about 1855. The steam ferry *Davenport,* left, went into service across the Mississippi in that year. Note that she is built on the conventional river-boat pattern like the steamer at right, rather than on the double-end style. The coach and horses are drawn up to leave the vessel on her starboard side, which is undoubtedly how she will go alongside the pier. There is a flatboat moving leisurely downstream, while the three men in the boat (foreground) are apparently working their own way across the river. The view is from Rock Island, Illinois.

points. Benjamin Miller did a thriving a business with his flatboat at Napoleon's Elbow on the Iowa. But the frontier was the Missouri. This was the jumping-off place, the last place where cash money was good, the place where people bought their outfits and gathered news and gossip of what lay ahead.

William Chick had one of the principal ferries across the Missouri at Kansas City; it had been a flatboat, but now it was horse-propelled. (Oddly enough, not a single steam ferry was yet operating anywhere on the Mississippi or the Missouri.) According to local legend, a traveling menagerie came to the ferry one day, and Chick managed to get the caged animals across without incident. But there was also an elephant which, at first, refused to have anything to do with the teamboat. The circus men finally got the elephant aboard, but Chick had to go to court to collect for damages done to his ferry.

There were many ferries across the Missouri, most of them concentrated along the hundred-odd miles where the river serves as the boundary between Missouri and Kansas. There was the ferry at Fort Leavenworth operated by Zadoc Martin, and another at Wyandotte, and there were Papan's, Smith's, Grinter's, and Marshall's. There was an Ogee's ferry, too, but I have been unable to discover whether this was owned by the same Joe Ogee who established the first ferry across the Rock River at Dixon, Illinois.

Joseph Boggs had a ferry not far from the mouth of the Kansas; before the Gold Rush he was charging $2 for a wagon and team. Other pre-1849 ferrymen were Richard Linville, John Thornton and Colonel Shubael Allen. Prime's Ferry was at Independence, Peter Roy's at Kansas City. Joseph Robidoux was a fur trader at St. Joseph, who also kept a ferry. It is likely that there were other ferries, too. In the vast confusion of the gold rush, a ferryman was anyone who owned a suitable boat, or could build one, and the ferry landing was anywhere a gold-seeker could go aboard.

The boom was incredible. At St. Joseph and other principal crossings, solid lines of wagons extended for miles back from the river front. Some were drawn by broken-down horses, some by oxen; many were clearly unequal to the journey. Some adventurers came on foot, pushing handcarts or laboring under heavy packs.

The official History of Buchanan County states: "During two and one-half months, from April 1 to June 15, 1849, the number of wagons that crossed there (St. Joseph) was 1,508, and averaging four men to a wagon would make 6,032. At Duncan's ferry, four miles above St. Joseph, 685 wagons crossed; at Bontown, Savannah and the ferries as far as the Bluffs, 2,000. This is a total of 4,193 wagons. About 10,000 crossed at Independence, making a total of 27,000 persons. There were about eight mules or oxen to each wagon."

Emigrants fought for places in line, offered large sums for an exchange of places, bribed the ferrymen. Some turned up or downstream to find another cross-

Council Bluffs, Iowa, 1853. Here are a group of Mormons awaiting passage across the Missouri into Nebraska. The flatboat is rowed by oarsmen.

ing, and considerable overflow business developed at a ferry pressed into service at old Fort Kearny, where the ferryman was Hiram P. Downs. Kanesville, which later became Council Bluffs, Iowa, had a good share of the traffic.

The maddest scenes, the panicky struggles to be first in California, had eased by 1850, though, statistically, emigration did not slacken. From this point on the pioneers were soberer and better prepared, and the gold-hunters were gradually replaced by people who might, if it looked promising, try their hand at prospecting, but who were chiefly interested in a place to live, a way of life, broad acres to own.

The journal of a California-bound traveler, John H. Clark, gives this colorful portrait of St. Joseph in 1852:

"We soon unloaded our goods and camped upon the plain just below the town. The whole neighborhood for miles around was full of emigrants, tents here and tents there, the white covers of wagons and tents looked as though they had been prepared for a grand army. And indeed they had been, for here were armies of men, with a goodly sprinkle of women and children. The city of St. Joe is much the gainer by the emigration. Thousands of dollars are spent here annually by those who cross the plains, it being one of the principal points where the emigration leaves the river.

"We here bought one yoke of oxen, a span of mules, and many other 'fixins' and made preparation for starting over the plains. There were hundreds of wagons waiting their turn for crossing the Missouri, and there were several boats busy, among them a steam ferryboat. But their capacity for carrying all the custom that presented itself was too small, and as a consequence there were many teams head of us in their turn.

"We supposed ourselves now ready for the trip and did not wish to remain any longer than possible [sic!]; were in quite a hurry to get off. After casting about endeavoring to see what was best, by accident came across a small flatboat which the owner was willing to hire, as he said, on reasonable terms.

"We got the boat, and now commenced the tug of war. 'Twas not Greek meets Greek, but the strife lay between the Saxon and the mule, for as fast as we got one devilish brute on board and our attention drawn to another, the first would jump overboard and swim ashore, to the great delight of the many who were looking on. After several turns of this kind, and finding that we advanced but slowly in our endeavors to freight the boat by the single addition, we concluded to drive them all in together 'pell-mell.' In this we succeeded admirably, and in they went, and we put up the bars to keep them there. A shout of victory followed the putting up of the railing. A victory was gained over the stubborn mule, and the order given to cast off, but before the order could be executed, the fiends in mule shape took it into their heads to all look over the same side of the boat, and at the same time, and the result was the careening of the boat so much to one side that it scared the little devils themselves, and they all, as with common consent, leaped overboard again. Three times three cheers was given by the crowd. So much fun could not pass unnoticed, or without applause . . ."

The accompanying illustration shows the ferry landing at Kansas City, on the western bank of the Missouri. Note the flatboat being poled across the stream and the river steamer headed down toward the Mississippi. The first steam ferry did not go into service on this part of the river until 1854, a year after this picture was drawn. The print was labeled simply, "Kansas—1853", and with it was the following legend:

"The bluff seen in the rear of the large buildings is an elevation of one hundred feet, leaving a spacious landing, with a rocky base, a wide street, and room for blocks of store-houses and other buildings. Toward the lower end of the town side, is a wide plain.

"The ox-team and large wagon seen approaching the ferry gives indication of one of the advantages of this town. It is one of the principal points on the Missouri for the outfit of caravans of traders and emigrants, on their journey over the plains and mountains, to the far-west.

"Here many thousands congregate in the spring season, to make preparations for their long line of march toward California, Salt Lake, New Mexico, and Oregon. Artisans supply them with wagons and gearing, stores furnish groceries and provisions, and farmers throughout the western part of Missouri are here with mules, horses, oxen, and cows, for their teams. Here, too, are found blacklegs, and other sharpers, with spotted bits of pasteboard, and other contrivances to filch the money and outfits from the wild and thoughtless . . ."

The first steam ferry to be put in service on the Missouri—and the reader will kindly insert the disclaimers and qualifications mentioned in earlier chapters— was the boat mentioned by John H. Clark at St. Joseph, the *Tidy Adala*. She ferried thousands across before a larger boat, the *Ebenezer*, replaced her in 1859. The *Tidy Adala* was then used for freight, but only for a few months, for she capsized and sank in 1860. The *Ebenezer* was commandeered in the Civil War and used as a gunboat.

In 1854 a Pittsburgh-built steam ferry was advertised in the *Kansas Weekly Herald*, published at Leavenworth:

"To Kansas Immigrants:

"STEAM FERRYBOAT. The undersigned announce with pleasure to all persons immigrating to Kansas, California, Oregon and Salt Lake City, that they have purchased a new, safe and commodious steam ferryboat, to ply between Weston and Fort Leavenworth. All persons who may wish to

NEW YORK PUBLIC LIBRARY, PHELPS STOKES COLLECTION

Kansas City, Kansas, 1853. Three men row the flatboat ferry across the Missouri River to the Missouri side of the stream. A small dog, attended by several people, watches from the bluff. It is not clear how wagons, animals, and passengers get from the high river bank onto the ferry. A river boat chuffs by in lordly indifference, headed downstream, perhaps to St. Louis. Notice her big wheels on the quarter, and the rudder directly aft.

cross the Missouri at this point, may rest assured that every exertion will be extended to them to insure a speedy and safe transit across the river. Call and try us.

"WELLS AND WASHBURN"

The newspaper commented that the boat was 126 feet long and had paddle wheels "that can knock all creation out of the river."

NEW YORK PUBLIC LIBRARY, PHELPS STOKES COLLECTION

Little Rock, Arkansas. This view, sketched just before the Civil War, shows what was probably the first steam ferry on the Arkansas River at this point. It looks remarkably like an Eastern double-ender. Two river freighters are on the other side of the river. Little Rock in this drawing resembles a university campus.

Several other steam ferries were introduced along the Missouri in the few years remaining before the Civil War. When that war ended, the bridge-building period began. It took time to build the bridges, and steam ferries remained in use here and there for several decades. But they came too late for the Gold Rush.

The map shows only seven ferries across the Missouri today, all but one upstream of Running Water, South Dakota. I do not wholly believe this, because there are so many places where there *ought* to be ferries, even if somewhat unofficial ones. Just south of Vermilion, South Dakota, for example, the map gives evidence that there was a ferry at some time in the past. Four miles from Vermilion, the dirt

"We found the ferries obstructed by masses of floating ice." [Page 208.]

Here is another frontier current ferry. Again the scene is dark; the season is winter. Ice obstructs the narrow stream. Everyone pulls to get the raft to shore, including the man in a top hat. That fellow with a pole apparently is shoving away the ice.

road dead-ends at the river bank. On the other side, roads from Maskell and Newcastle, Nebraska join and dead-end at an opposite point. To cross at the Yankton or Sioux City bridges would require fifty miles or more of extra driving. Surely people living near Maskell have a way of crossing.

But the remaining ferries are all marginal; none are on main roads. Wherever the settlers crossed, the Big Mo is now bridged.

Songs and Sorrows

≈≈≈≈≈≈≈≈≈≈≈≈≈≈≈≈≈≈≈≈≈≈≈≈≈≈≈≈≈≈≈≈

Chapter Thirteen

In the history of the ferryboat, a most significant day is June 29, 1814. For on that evening the Brooklyn steam ferry *Nassau* was withdrawn from her usual run to take 250 passengers on an excursion. Under a bright moon, decked with lanterns and with a band playing, the *Nassau* cruised up the East River almost to Hell Gate, turned and sailed downstream, around Whitehall and up the North River, turned again and chuffed to the Battery, where she paused to serenade the people ashore. Then she stood out into the bay, circled Governor's Island, and returned to her slip.

An excursion! Small wonder Brooklynites were thrilled and exuberant. For until that time the crossing from Brooklyn to Manhattan had been difficult, often dangerous and uncomfortable, and too frequently fatal. Winter ice and summer squalls had taken a heavy toll of lives, and crossing in a dead calm was likely to mean blistered palms, for passengers were obliged to help at the oars.

Up to now the ferryhouse had been the attraction, a place of warmth and cheer. The ferry itself, however, was anything but that. The *Nassau's* cruise betokened a new day.

It was a giant forward step. John Stevens took the next when he launched the *Pioneer* in 1825, with a ladies' cabin, heated and carpeted, and mirrors on the walls. No longer was the ferry strictly utilitarian; each succeeding vessel was larger, more luxurious, more of a joy to the traveler.

So, quite soon, the ferry was celebrated in song. One of the songsters was George W. Osborn of Detroit, who composed this lyric about 1840:

132

RIDING ON THE FERRY

When the mercury denotes
    Sultry summer heat,
Then the spacious ferry-boats
    Afford a cool retreat,
On a shady upper deck,
    Joined by friends so merry,
Bless me! ain't it pleasant,
    Riding on the ferry?

Back and forth from shore to shore,
    On the rippling river,
Watching spray beads rise and fall,
    Where the sunbeams quiver;
Reveling in the cooling breeze,
    Every one is cheery;
Bless me! ain't it pleasant,
    Riding on the ferry?

Now you're sitting vis-a-vis
    With a charming creature,
Happiness is in her eye,
    Joy in every feature.
"Isn't this superb?" she asks,
    "Yes," you answer, "very."
Bless me! ain't it pleasant,
    Riding on the ferry?

Thus the heated hours are passed,—
    Laughing, joking, singing;
Joyous shouts from happy groups
    On the cool breeze ringing.
Now you see your charmer home,
    Feeling blithe and merry,
'Cause engaged to go tomorrow
    Riding on the ferry.

At first it was an adventure comparable to a ride in a Jenny or a Waco bi-plane a century later. It was every bit as novel, to feel the deck of a boat rumble and throb underfoot, to hear the hissing and chuffing and clanking, to see the big

Charleston, South Carolina, 1838. This view of Charleston from across the Cooper River shows one of the earliest steam ferries. Charleston is at the confluence of two rivers, the Ashley and the Cooper. Notice the man with the bright button eyes in the foreground, searching intently for something; the topsail schooner hove to in midstream; and the mixed bag of steamers and sailing vessels in the river.

paddle wheels dipping into the water and the foaming wake astern. There was some of the same spice of danger, too, for fires and boiler explosions were not uncommon.

But people everywhere accepted the steam ferries at once, and took them to their hearts; for there the ferry was, right at the landing at the end of the street, and for a pittance anyone could walk aboard. The whole family could ride, and neighbors, too. In a moment or so the lines were cast off, the whistle blew, and

THE NEW-YORK HISTORICAL SOCIETY, NEW YORK CITY

Charleston, South Carolina. This view said to be of the ferry and ferry landing at Charleston, is otherwise unidentified. It is probably a crossing of the Ashley River and the date is about 1840. The sail on the right-hand sloop seems to be collapsing. That is a formidable smokestack for so small a ferryboat.

there you were out in the channel amidst the big steamers, the many-masted schooners and the tall square-riggers.

Once the ferryman had been a commonplace, loquacious fellow, who pulled an oar or leaned on a tiller. Now the ferry had a full-fledged captain like a proper ship, aloof from his passengers in the pilot house, lordly as could be in his uniform. Some captains tried to imitate the ways of Commodore Cornelius Vanderbilt, who stalked the upper deck alone like a Roman emperor, pounding the deck with his cane to telegraph his orders to the engine-room.

Not all steam ferries were splendid, to be sure. The Kottmeyers of Kentucky were typical of numerous enterprising ferrymen who bought some kind of steam

THE MARINERS' MUSEUM, NEWPORT NEWS, VIRGINIA

Boston, 1833. This is the East Boston ferry, with stars and screaming eagle on the paddle box. The ships in the background appear to be drying their sails.

engine, often one built for quite a different purpose, set it in a home-made hull, and experimented with walking beams, cranks and paddle wheels until they had something which would cross the river. One candid operator advertised: "We have two boats. When one don't work, the other will."

But at New York, Philadelphia, Boston, Detroit, and other major cities, and at the principal crossings of the Hudson, Delaware, Schuylkill, and other important rivers, the ferry quickly took on its familiar modern form: double-ended, to facilitate loading and unloading, passenger cabins at either side, projecting well out beyond the hull, pilot houses above. Upper decks were soon added to accommodate more passengers.

Now the builders tried to out-do each other in elaborate appointments. The big pre-Civil War ferries were ornamented with carved wood and cast metal. There were benches made of well-seasoned walnut by fine cabinet-makers, beautifully fitted together, sanded smooth and varnished until they shone. There were windows and mirrors and sliding doors, and even grand stairways to the upper deck. The *Dido*, built for the Camden-Philadelphia run, had a calliope but the first time they tried it the horses on board became panicky, and it took the better part of an hour to untangle the cat's cradle of wheels, tongues, and harness.

Local trade was the chief support of the city ferries by the middle nineteenth century, and business was good. So, again, competition became vigorous on some crossings. The Supreme Court decision in the case of Gibbons vs. Ogden had broken the monopoly, but the federal government had not undertaken to regulate ferries, even inter-state services.* So the old conflict of jurisdiction remained.

At Philadelphia, the Camden and Philadelphia Steamboat Ferry Company had an idea. As the illustration in Chapter VII shows, Windmill Island lay between Camden and Philadelphia, forcing ferries to make a dog-leg course. This group of ferry operators approached the Pennsylvania legislature and were granted permission to cut a channel through the island.

They had hoped to have it for their very own and were disgusted in the extreme when the legislature required them to keep the channel open to all. But they would be permitted to exact tolls from all other users, and since the tolls were not fixed they thought it worth while to go ahead.

After a time the channel was all cut and ready, but the proprietors, though using it themselves, failed to announce any public opening. Indeed, they ordered competitors' boats to stay out of the channel.

The competitors promptly went into court. But court decisions would take some time to obtain, so meanwhile the enterprising ferrymen slashed their fares. With the lowest fares on the river *and* the quickest service, they might have been able to force a settlement. But one firm, the West Jersey Ferry Company, coun-

* The Interstate Commerce Commission did not come into existence until 1887.

tered by ordering their boats to use the channel anyway, and refused to ask permission or pay the toll. So another lawsuit went to court.

This went on for some time, but before it was settled, both ferry companies were brought under the control of the Pennsylvania Railroad. So no decision was necessary. The case would have become moot eventually, anyway, for the island has long since disappeared.

One of the worst ferry tragedies in American history had its beginning in this controversial channel. It happened on the night of March 15, 1856. The steam ferry *New Jersey*, running as the only night boat, left Walnut Street, Philadelphia, about 8 P.M. The river was full of floating ice, and the ferry had rough going, so all hands were relieved when she finally pulled into the shelter of the channel.

But she was no sooner in the channel when someone cried, "Fire!" A moment later the flames broke through the deck, around the stack.

The captain signaled for hard astern, she backed, and taking advantage of

the incoming tide he managed to swing her and make way back toward the Philadelphia shore. His best chance now was the Arch Street slip, and he drove her through the ice under full power. She almost made it. Indeed, the *New Jersey's* bow made contact briefly with the wharf. But at that moment flames swept into the pilot house and swirled through the engine room, and drove both captain and crew out. From that moment the vessel was dead in the water. Before a line could be tossed, the tide caught her in the ice and spun the blazing, passenger-laden craft out to mid-stream.

Many of the passengers burned to death. Others leaped to the ice, or into the water. Only a few managed to reach shore. There were sixty known dead.

Now the lawyers' long battle of jurisdiction was renewed. Coroners' juries met in both Camden and Philadelphia. The Philadelphia jury concluded that the deaths were a result of criminal negligence by the company, a New Jersey corporation, in that the ferry was unfit for the transportation of passengers.

But nothing came of this, for the Camden prosecutor had taken the precau-

Brooklyn, 1845. This view over the East River is from the U. S. Hotel in lower Manhattan. In the foreground is the Fulton Ferry slip, with a boat just departing. The Brooklyn slip is at the left, just at the bend. Notice how Brooklyn, even with big buildings, is still a small community crouching by the water's edge. Church steeples are by far the tallest structures in the town, rivalled only by the trees covering the hills in the background. The white steamers heading up-river are bound for New England ports. All have walking beams and paddle wheels. The three-masted sailing ship to the left of the ferry appears to be backing out slowly. There is a four-masted paddle-steamer headed out to sea at the right.

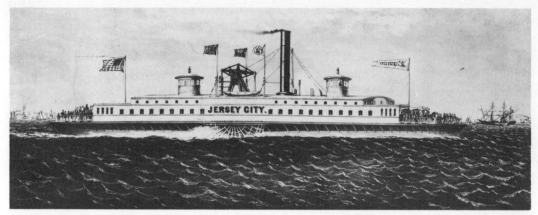

A Hudson River boat, 1862. This handsome lithograph shows the *Jersey City,* owned by the New Jersey Rail Road & Transportation Company. This 206-foot sidewheeler was first on the Jersey City to Cortland Street run, later on the Lackawanna's Hoboken service. Her dimensions, typical enough of a ferryboat, are interesting, with a beam of 34 feet 6 inches, extended by the paddle wheels and cabins to 63 feet. The depth of hold (from main deck to keel) was 18 feet, and the diameter of the wheels was 22 feet. This picture shows clearly the walking beam, which rocked up and down far above the great engine.

The destruction by fire of the steam ferry *New Jersey* on the Delaware between Philadelphia and Camden in March, 1856. Many of the passengers have climbed onto ice floes to save themselves, but for some it was no use. Over fifty died, most probably from drowning or freezing.

tion of arresting all of the officers and directors of the company, holding them for New Jersey justice—and the Camden Grand Jury refused to indict. The affair ended in a welter of violent newspaper editorials and pamphlets.

Fortunately many of the fires and explosions occurred while ferries were in their slips. But there were disasters in the channel, and in some of them loss of life might have been averted by the presence of even one working fire-hose, or a lifeboat, or a few life-preservers. Yet not until the Civil War were ferries and their officers brought within the provisions of a federal Steamboat Inspection Act.

It was that great war that checked for a time the development of steam ferry service. When the war broke, there were, perhaps, as many as 150 steam ferries in use in the United States, serving now from coast to coast. But in the war some ferries were halted by hostilities. Others went off to fight.

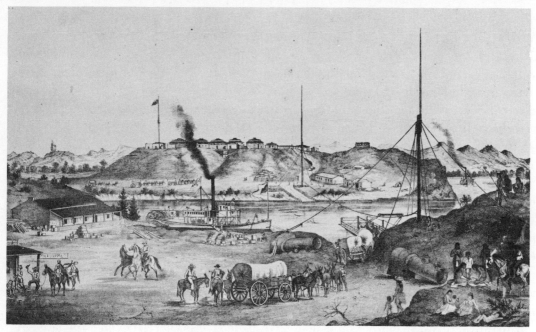

CHICAGO HISTORICAL SOCIETY

Fort Yuma, California. This illustration shows a current ferry crossing the Colorado River from the site of present-day Yuma, Arizona, to the California side. It is undated. Not far distant is the Mexican border. Notice the two stern-wheel steamers (one going up-river at the right) and the two steam boilers lying on the shore. The ferry cable must have been a considerable handicap to local river traffic. It is not clear whether it was lowered to the river bottom when ships wished to pass or raised above them, suspended from the two masts on opposite shores.

Amateur Warships: Ferryboats in the Civil War

~~~~~~

CHAPTER FOURTEEN

WHITE MEN HAVE USED ferryboats in America for more than four hundred years. Thousands of boats have been used, some crude, some splendid. Comedies and tragedies have been played on the decks of these ferries. People have died, have loved, have hatched great plans, and have lost fortunes between shores. Ferries have carried great men and humble, at critical moments and at dull times. There have been times of adventure and occasions of danger, but always in that rigid framework, always in the course of the ferry's mission of shuttling endlessly between fixed points.

Yet there came, suddenly, unexpectedly, a long day of glory for the American ferryboat. At the time of the Nation's need, in the War between the States, the ferryboat suddenly became an instrument of power. The ferry was taken from its quiet routine and became a warship; not an auxiliary, but a full member of the fleet which went into battle, flags flying and guns ablaze.

As North and South reviewed their assets and strategies, it was plain that control of the seas and inland waterways would have much to do with the outcome of their conflict. The opposing sides had been interdependent for raw materials and manufactures, so both would now have to look elsewhere, beyond the seas. A great many naval officers had resigned their regular commissions and accepted those granted by the South, but they had not brought their warships with them. As a result the South, when the war began, had virtually no navy. Thus there was no likelihood that the South could blockade Northern ports. But, at the same time, the Northern navy was far from large enough to patrol the entire Atlantic and Gulf coasts.

Inland waterways might, in the long run, be even more important than the oceans. Much of the commerce of both North and South was water-borne. Railroad mileage was increasing, but important links were missing; indeed, railroads were

142

not yet equal competitors with river steamers or coastal vessels, and in few cases had railroad builders dared to parallel the water highways. Nor were wagon trains a fraction as effective as steamboats between points on a navigable waterway. For civilian and military supply alike, the rivers flowing down into the Atlantic and the Gulf, and above all, the immense system of the Mississippi Valley, were indispensable. Sooner or later, control of the rivers would mean victory in the war.

The United States Navy consisted of about ninety wooden ships. The latest and best of them were three-masted sailing vessels provided with a steam engine driving a single propeller. On the open sea they were the equals of anything afloat, fast enough to overhaul and subdue merchant ships, powerful enough to overcome most foreign warships. In support of armies their huge batteries could pour a heavy fire of grape, cannister, or ball into enemy troops and strong points.

But they had not been designed for fighting on the inland waterways of their own country. Here the need was for maneuverable vessels of shallow draft, ships of small size. The United States Navy had few such vessels. The only way to get them in time was to commandeer or purchase commercial river and harbor boats.

By the end of 1861 the Navy had so acquired 136 privately-owned steamers, and that was but the beginning. Many of these were ferryboats. How many ferries there were altogether no one seems to know, for in the Navy Register most of them appear simply as vessels of the fourth class, together with other types of comparable size. However, we do know that 22 double-ended ferries fought for the Union cause.

One of the 22 was the *Commodore Perry* of New York. The old photograph reproduced here shows how she was converted to the Navy's uses. The pilot house was lightly armored, heavy guns were mounted on the open deck, and iron plates were set up to give some protection to the men at the guns.

It was a simple conversion, but it was enough to make the ferry a fighting ship of considerable potency. Like the other steam ferries a sidewheeler, the *Commodore Perry* was quite vulnerable to gunfire or ramming. On the other hand, sidewheelers were more maneuverable than propeller ships. Members of the armed boarding parties—boarding was the normal way of capturing enemy vessels—could remain under cover, relatively safe from musket fire. The *Commodore Perry* was fast, more highly maneuverable than most ships, and of shallow enough draft to nose into shore almost anywhere. She could quickly take aboard a striking force of cavalry or infantry, and, without having to "back" away, steam off to set them ashore on the enemy's unprotected flank. Such craft, predecessors of our present-day infantry landing ships, provided the Northern troops with a priceless mobility and so reduced enormously the number of soldiers necessary for a successful campaign.

Another of the ferries used in this manner was the *Delaware*, also shown here, which took part in Major General Ambrose Burnside's expedition to North Carolina in 1861-1862. As shown in our illustration, the *Delaware* was at this time neither armed nor armored, though written accounts say she carried two heavy guns. In any event, Commodore Stephen C. Rowan chose her as his flagship for operations in the North Carolina sounds—partly for her shallow draft and maneuverability, and partly because there was no better ship available.

The extensive but shallow sounds along the Carolina coast were an important theater of naval warfare. Albemarle and Pamlico sounds and their numberless

The United States 4th Rate Steamer *Commodore Perry*. Purchased for the Federal Navy in October, 1861, for $38,000, this 512-ton wooden sidewheeler measured 143 feet in length, drew 10 feet of water, and was capable of a sluggish 7 knots. After the war (in which $56,000 were spent in repairs) she was sold back to New York ferry interests for $16,200. The two big shell guns in this picture are Dahlgren smoothbores. Notice their large crews, drawn up as for inspection. The thin iron plates surrounding the guns and around the pilot house could be raised to protect the men against splinters and infantry shot. The *Perry* took part in several vigorously-fought actions in North Carolina waters.

tributary rivers gave the Confederates, potentially, a salt-water stronghold, easy to defend with fortifications and small naval forces at the few channels through the outer banks and islands. The sounds and rivers also interrupted the main coastal highways time and again.

But the Confederate Navy was too weak to keep safe the key positions. On August 29, 1861, a small Federal squadron under Flag Officer Silas Stringham attacked and captured forts Clark and Hatteras, opening the sounds to Northern penetration.

The opening was not exploited until January, 1862. By then it had become urgent, for the Confederates were building ironclads in these waters, vessels which could destroy any Union ship then afloat. So, a Federal expedition set out to sweep the sounds. On January 12 the fleet, composed largely of former ferryboats, arrived off Hatteras. Several days later it sailed north through Pamlico Sound to seek control of the narrow channel at Roanoke Island which leads to Albemarle Sound.

This was to be a coordinated amphibious operation, with Flag Officer Louis Goldsborough commanding the naval forces and General Burnside the army. Against weak Southern resistance it succeeded wonderfully. Commodore Lynch's smaller Confederate squadron (also made up of makeshift warships) was unable to stem Federal strikes at forts Barstow and Blanchard. While part of the Federal ferry flotilla engaged the forts, other vessels put troops ashore to the number of 15,000. They swept up behind the guns and both strongholds were forced to surrender.

Now Rowan, in command of Goldsborough's ferryboats, took off into Albemarle Sound in pursuit of the Confederate squadron, which withdrew up the Pasquotank River toward Elizabeth City. Lynch made his final stand at Fort Cobb, but it was a futile one. Rowan's ferryboat squadron, including both the *Delaware* and the *Commodore Perry*, attacked, and Lynch's force was virtually destroyed. The eventual result of this operation, some months later, was the recapture by the North of Norfolk, Virginia. This in turn forced the destruction by its own crew of the dread Confederate ironclad *Merrimac*.

Rowan's operations at the southern extremity of the sounds were similarly successful, though less dramatic. Our picture of the ferryboat *Delaware* shows an apparently peaceful scene on the Neuse River. The Tenth Connecticut Regiment is on the north shore at about the point where the old ferry crossed, on what is now U. S. Route 17. Across the river is New Bern, North Carolina.

Of the ferries that fought in the Civil War, perhaps the most distinguished was the *Westfield*, one of several taken from the Staten Island run. She was of the walking-beam and paddle wheel variety, quite handy, but vulnerable. This prosaic little vessel made the long voyage down the Atlantic coast, around the Florida keys, and through the Gulf of Mexico. In April, 1862, she was in Flag Officer David

U.S.S. *Delaware*. Purchased at Wilmington, Delaware, in October, 1861, this iron sidewheeler was rated at 13 knots, drew only 6 feet of water. Differently armed at various times, she seems, during the Neuse River operation shown here, to have carried two or three guns of assorted types and sizes. According to the original caption those people in the foreground belonged to the Tenth Connecticut Regiment awaiting transportation to New Berne, North Carolina, across the river.

THE CIVIL WAR IN THE UNITED STATES

Farragut's supporting force when he and his fleet crossed the bar and entered the Mississippi River.

A short time earlier the capture of forts Henry and Donelson by General Grant and Flag Officer Foote had opened up the Tennessee and Cumberland rivers to Northern penetration and forced the Confederates on the Mississippi to fall back to a new defense based on Island Number 10, near Tiptonville, Tennessee. On the

The *Westfield* performs a courageous act. A Southern fire raft has been sent to drift down upon Farragut's war fleet anchored in the lower Mississippi. The *Westfield,* one of Commodore Vanderbilt's old New York ferries, shoves the blazing raft away from the anchored warships, all the while playing her firehose on the flames. In this picture ships' boats are rowing out to help the ferry. Notice how the artist couldn't agree with himself on the direction the wind was blowing.

night of April 4 Commander Henry Walke with the United States ironclad gunboat *Carondelet* ran past the island fortress, followed two nights later by another ironclad, the *Pittsburg*. This made the Southern position untenable, and their forces evacuated, opening the river down to Fort Pillow, near Memphis.

The Confederates were still in control downstream, but when the news came of Farragut's arrival at the mouth of the Mississippi the commanding officer at

FRANK LESLIE'S FAMOUS LEADERS AND BATTLE SCENES OF THE CIVIL WAR

New Orleans asked for more support—which could only be drawn from Fort Pillow and other forces in Tennessee. Help was, at first, denied, but in the West in the spring of '62 it made little difference where the Confederates put their strength: they could only choose where they would first meet defeat.

New Orleans' main defense against Farragut's fleet consisted of Fort Jackson and Fort St. Philip, on opposite shores of the Mississippi and about seventy-five miles downstream from the city. Immediately below the forts a chain was stretched across the river, supported by hulks. It was a barrier not sufficient in itself, but it might delay the Federal ships as they moved upstream against the current long enough to expose them to fatal blows from the forts.

On April 18 the *Westfield* performed a useful and courageous service. That night Farragut's ships were at anchor in the river below the forts. Sails were furled, fires low beneath the boilers. Up-river, around the bend, the Confederates had secretly built a huge raft. Now they piled it high with wood, with brush, and with

THE CIVIL WAR IN THE UNITED STATES

Ferryboats with the fleet in the Mississippi. This sketch, rendered a few days before Farragut's great dash to New Orleans, shows the Federal fleet resting below the Confederate forts guarding the city. On the left Commander David Porter's mortar boats are opening their long bombardment. The ships at bottom left are three gunboats, then the ferryboat *Jackson,* the

other inflammables. They ignited it and set the monster adrift, roaring with flames. Union sailors on watch cried alarm as they saw the great fiery thing come down upon them and their powerless ships.

The *Westfield* still had steam up and it was she who responded to the crisis. Her captain cut loose her anchor and headed the ferryboat boldly toward the flaming mass, while sailors broke out the fire hose. Seeing that the raft was headed directly toward one of the anchored warships, the *Westfield's* skipper rammed the raft, and with flames scorching his paint and woodwork, shoved it away from the helpless vessel. Then he backed off, staying just close enough for his fire hose to reach. By now longboats from the other ships had come to help with buckets and boat hooks. Together they and the *Westfield* guided the fire raft past the long line of anchored ships and then let it drift off harmlessly into the night.

The next morning Farragut began to bombard the forts. It was to last for five days and five nights. Our picture shows the Federal ships going into action.

Mississippi, the *Pensacola,* and the *Hartford.* The last-named is actually the same size as the *Pensacola,* and not much bigger than the side-wheeled *Mississippi.* The mastless vessel in the group of four to the right is the ferry *Westfield.* The others are the *Iroquois, Cayuga,* and *Varuna.*

THE PICTORIAL BATTLES OF THE CIVIL WAR, 1885

The end of the *Westfield*. On New Year's Day, 1863, the *Westfield* was destroyed by her skipper to keep her out of Southern hands after she had been grounded under the guns of the Confederate squadron at Galveston, Texas. A big ferry, she had cost the Navy $90,000 when purchased from Commodore Vanderbilt in the fall of 1861. The 215-foot *Westfield* carried six heavy guns.

The largest of those in the drawing, near the center, is Farragut's flagship *Hartford*. Three from the left of the flagship is the ferryboat *Jackson*. The *Westfield* is in the group of four to the right. The hulks supporting the Confederate chain can be seen at the narrows. Fort Jackson is beyond the point at the left, Fort St. Philip opposite, and the Confederate defense fleet beyond.

About 2 A.M. on April 24 Farragut's fleet steamed up between the forts. The darkness was full of flame and thunder, but with the dawn the fleet was past. Five big ships and a number of smaller vessels made the dash, but neither the *Westfield* nor the *Jackson* were among them. With but one exception all the ships the great admiral took with him that night were regular men-of-war. The next day Farragut was off New Orleans and the city was his.

Other engagements were still to be fought upstream, but, except around Vicksburg, Confederate resistance was more brave than effective. After their success at Island Number 10 the ironclads moved downriver to Fort Pillow. There they met an initial check by the Southern river defense fleet. But the Northern flotilla forced another battle, off Memphis on June 6, in which all but one of the eight Confederate ships were sunk or captured. The city of Memphis surrendered immediately to become, for a time, General Grant's headquarters.

The *Westfield's* last adventure came a few months later, on New Year's Day, 1863. This time it was at Galveston, Texas, which the Federals had seized and garrisoned with a small force. Major General J. Bankhead Magruder of the Confederacy planned a coordinated land and sea assault, with Commodore Smith commanding the Southern naval arm.

Union soldiers had erected heavy barricades to defend the city. Magruder's first move was to send troops forward, seeking to get around the barricades by wading through shallow water. They were seen by the small Federal flotilla and Commander William B. Renshaw, who commanded the Northern naval force from the *Westfield*, moved his ships into position to fire on the foe. Under his command that day were two other gunboats, the *Owasco* and the *Clifton*, the latter a running-mate of the *Westfield* on the old Staten Island service.

They poured a withering fire into Magruder's troops, who fell back, seeking safety. But at this instant Commodore Smith's gunboats entered the battle. They attacked another of Renshaw's ships, the revenue cutter *Harriet Lane*. Two Southern gunboats closed in, one on either side. The Federals disabled one of them, but the other, the *Bayou City*, drove hard into the *Harriet Lane's* paddle wheel, locking with her. The *Bayou City's* sailors swarmed over the side and the *Harriet Lane's* crew surrendered. The *Owasco* charged in, either to retake the *Harriet Lane* or to sink her, but she was driven off by heavy fire from the captured guns.

Meanwhile other Confederate gunboats had attacked the *Westfield* and driven her aground. Commodore Smith now sent a flag signal to Renshaw, demanding that he surrender the whole fleet, and gave him three hours to consider. Renshaw agreed to consider the proposal, and all Union ships ran up white flags (to indicate a truce) and anchored.

Shortly before the three-hour period would have ended, Smith addressed another message to Renshaw: Surrender at once all Union ships under Confederate guns; leave to later negotiation the fate of the others. But while this message was on the way, the *Westfield* blew up.

Accounts agree that she was destroyed to keep her from falling into Confederate hands. But some say that Renshaw deliberately blew up himself and his crew, while others believe this part of the sacrifice was accidental.

Eyewitnesses also differ on what followed. Confederate sources say the remaining Union ships attempted to steam off, still flying white flags. Northerners deny this. In any case, the Confederate ships opened fire again. Another Federal ship was sunk, the *Owasco* was heavily damaged, and two barks and a schooner were captured.

The Union garrison, holding an isolated city far from help, now found its lifeline cut by this Confederate success. Their position was a hopeless one; they surrendered, and Galveston returned to Confederate control until the end of the war.

The ferryboat *Clifton* managed to escape from this disaster. The following September 8 she participated in an ill-conceived attempt to seize Sabine City, Texas.

Sabine Pass controls the entrance to Lake Sabine, Port Arthur, and the Sabine River, boundary between Louisiana and Texas. Taking it was a good idea, and, once again, the plan was to do it by combined military and naval forces. Union intelligence should have been good, for the city had been in Federal hands just the year before. But something went badly astray.

The idea, apparently, was to silence the batteries at Sabine Pass by naval gunfire. Then the flotilla would move in and land troops. But, to silence the batteries, only three boats went forward, the ferry *Clifton* and two even smaller gunboats, the *Sachem* and the *Arizona*.

About a hundred sharpshooters were put on board the vessels to try to pick off enemy gunners, while cannon on both vessels blasted away. They came in bravely, and—for a brief moment—it seemed that they might succeed, for the shore batteries were strangely silent. But it was a silence of contempt, not of resignation. The gunners on shore took their time, aimed carefully, waited until all targets were well within range. Then the shore guns all let go at once, and that ended the show. Struck time and again, her biggest gun wrecked and her boiler pierced, the *Clifton* drifted aground; she was forced to surrender. At the same time the *Sachem* was so crippled she, too, had to strike her colors. Only the *Arizona* escaped. A fourth gunboat never entered the fray.

THE MARINERS' MUSEUM, NEWPORT NEWS, VIRGINIA

The disabling and capture of the *Clifton* in the attack on Sabine Pass, Texas, on September 8, 1863. The *Clifton,* the *Sachem* (at right), and the *Arizona* attacked the enemy forts at Sabine Pass to prepare the way for a landing by Northern troops. The *Clifton* was damaged and went aground. She continued the fight for a while but the damage mounted and she was forced to strike her colors. The *Sachem* surrendered too, but the *Arizona* escaped. An 892-ton sidewheeler, the *Clifton* in 1863 carried two heavy guns and four lighter weapons of assorted types, including one army gun. The *Sachem* was a propeller-driven vessel, apparently built for fishing or local trade.

The Georgetown Ferry during the Civil War. This current ferry, crossing the Potomac at Georgetown, was under control of the Union army, with soldiers guarding both landings. Only those with passes could cross. The ferry barge is quite large and seems very substantial. The sturdy bridge in the background appears to be for the railroad. To possess the local ferries and bridges is one of the primary aims of a campaigning army, whether it be advancing or retreating.

There are many more stories about the Civil War ferry-gunboats, tales of desperate fights, of victory and of defeat. But they are tales which belong more properly in naval histories. We must note, though, that all these stories are of Federal ferryboats. Nowhere could I find a positive record of a converted ferry serving the Confederacy. The South used many small river steamers, but these were largely stern-wheelers. There seem to have been no double-enders in Confederate service.

By the end of 1863 the Federal Navy had built a great many small warships especially designed for river and coastal war. As they entered service, they replaced the makeshift ferryboat-warships. The ferries did perform some useful combat service well into the next year, supporting General Grant's army in Virginia, but that was all. Of the twenty-two double-enders, seventeen survived the perils and adventures of war.

In Days Gone By

CHAPTER FIFTEEN

WHEN THE CIVIL WAR was over the ferryboats went back to their ordinary tasks. They would never again be used in battle, for by the the time of the Spanish-American War the development of ships of war was too far advanced. (Even so, the Navy purchased two ferryboats in 1898, one in Boston, the other at Norfolk. The first one never left home. The second failed to get past Cape Hatteras and spent the rest of the war behind the guns of Fortress Monroe.)

The steam ferry had now taken on its characteristic shape, one little different from the steam ferries that have been built since. Railroads boomed after the Civil War and in a number of cities ferries served as links between rail terminals on opposite shores. As rail service improved, it soon became practical for people who worked in cities to live outside them. Thus was born the American commuter.

I became a commuter on the first Monday in December, 1934. From my home in Maplewood, New Jersey, it was a brisk walk to the Lackawanna Station. Usually I could hear the train coming as I quick-stepped through the tunnel below the tracks.

"Why do you ride the Lackawanna?" began an ancient vaudeville wheeze. The snapper was: "Because it passes around the Oranges every morning." The 7:29, my train, was an express, speeding through the Oranges to its first stop at Newark, then across the meadows to the Hoboken Terminal.

The Delaware, Lackawanna & Western Railroad ("Delay, Linger & Wait" to its friends) leased the terminal and its ferries in 1904; it had previously acquired the Morris & Essex rail lines that gave it access to the port of New York. The ferries were operating at capacity then, and the old ferry terminal was woefully inadequate.

Fall River, Massachusetts. This print was not identified, but it dates from between 1866, when the big Fall River steamer *Bristol* was built, and 1888 when she burned. The double-ended ferry *Oriole* was completed in 1864. Notice her paddle wheels and walking beam, as well as the already-industrialized character of the city behind her. The stream is the Taunton River, which empties into Narragansett Bay, and then into the Atlantic.

THE MARINERS' MUSEUM, NEWPORT NEWS, VIRGINIA

New York City, 1866. The ferry business was booming. Passengers at the Barclay Street landing of the Hoboken Ferry have swarmed aboard the *Morristown* and are blocking the way to prevent teams from boarding. From *Frank Leslie's Illustrated Newspaper,* March 10, 1866.

FRANK LESLIE'S ILLUSTRATED NEWSPAPER, MARCH 10, 1866

Walking-beam-and-paddle wheel ferries were still in service although the last two boats of this variety built for the Hoboken Ferry were the *Montclair* and *Orange*, delivered from the shipyards in 1885. They were still sound in the early 1930's, when new boilers were installed, and I rode on them often before they were sold to a salvage company in 1944.

Screw propulsion was not unknown in the 1880's; Stevens' *Little Juliana*, built in 1804, had twin propellers, and many boats using screw propulsion had been built before the Stevens family drew up their specifications for the *Montclair* and *Orange*. They thought of using it, and built at least one model, but in the end decided to rely on the known qualities of the paddle-wheel. A propeller was simple to apply in a conventional boat, for the engine could be mounted at an angle, so the shaft would slant downward to the stern. In a double-ended vessel, this could not be done; using two engines, one for each end, was suggested, but that was clearly not practical, and transmitting power from one engine through universal joints would introduce still other problems.

One other way remained: a single engine with horizontal shafts. At first, this seemed to present an insuperable handicap: the propellers would lie too shallowly. This was the solution ultimately adopted, however, when the Stevenses' first big propeller-driven boat, the *Bergen*, was built at Newburgh in 1888.* She had a single shaft, running the entire length of the vessel, with a propeller at each end, so that one pushed while the other pulled. The direction of travel was changed by reversing the engine.

The *Bergen* was 203 feet long, 62 feet in the beam, and equipped with gas lights. The elimination of the paddle-wheels gave more space for passengers. She was a big success, faster and easier to handle than the paddle-wheel ferries, and she set the new pattern.

The problem of the obsolete ferryhouse adjusted itself on the night of August 7, 1905, shortly after the Lackawanna took over. At about eleven o'clock, Captain William Berton of the ferry *Musconetcong* was in his pilot house making log entries, while passengers were coming aboard below. Startled by a sudden glow, he looked up and saw flames spurting around the base of the stack of the ferry *Hopatcong* in the next slip. Berton grabbed his whistle cord and blew the fire alarm, then immediately whistled to his deck hands to cast off. His intention was to get a line on the *Hopatcong* and tow her away from shore, but it was already too late. Even as he pulled out of his slip, the ferry shed caught fire.

Out in the river the tug *Idlewild* was towing a string of barges, and her captain, too, saw the blaze. He dropped his tow and steamed in to help. One of

* A year earlier another propeller-driven double-ender, the *Silver Gate,* was launched at Coronado, California. But she proved a failure and after a few weeks she was set aside to become a floating dance-palace.

FRANK LESLIE'S ILLUSTRATED NEWSPAPER, DECEMBER 15, 1866

Burning of the ferryboat *Idaho*. "A disaster which has long been predicted by those acquainted with the way in which our ferries are managed has just occurred. The illustrations which accompany this will give our readers some idea of the awful scene which was presented on Monday evening, the 26th of November, by the burning of the ferryboat *Idaho* while crossing from Brooklyn to New York. The excitement which prevailed on both shores while the boat was to be seen on fire, and no one knew how many lives were in peril, or what means those unfortunate persons on board had for escaping, was terrible to witness. Providentially no lives were lost, but everyone shudders to think what would have happened, if, instead of only thirty or forty people on board, when the fire broke out, there had been, as is not unusual, between six and eight hundred which number, it may be observed, there would certainly have been when the boat was returning on the same trip from the New York side. It is safe to say that in the horrid confusion that would have arisen, very few could have escaped a miserable death. We may thank God that we have been spared such a catastrophe."—*Frank Leslie's Illustrated Newspaper*, December 15, 1866.

FRANK LESLIE'S ILLUSTRATED NEWSPAPER, DECEMBER 15, 1866

James O'Neil, engineer of the *Idaho,* prepares to leap over-board with one of the lady passengers in his arms.

FRANK LESLIE'S ILLUSTRATED NEWSPAPER, DECEMBER 15, 1866

O'Neil, the rescued lady, and other passengers are pulled from the icy water. The rescue boat is called a yawl.

his crew undertook the hazardous task of getting a line on the *Hopatcong*, by then a blazing torch. The heat was so intense his shipmates had to douse him with a hose, but he managed to get the line across to the burning vessel and tied fast. The *Montclair*, approaching Hoboken from New York, came in to help, and together she and the tug got the *Hopatcong* out. The fire by now was utterly uncontrollable, so they towed the flaming ferry to the Weehawken flats, where she burned to the water's edge. The *Binghamton*, also ablaze, had been pulled out of her slip by now, but this fire was brought under control and, though badly damaged, she was saved.

On shore, the fire spread so quickly there was no stopping it. Since the fire began on the water side, land-based firemen could not take up strategic positions. It would have done little good anyway, a few thin streams of water hissing into an ocean of flame. Heat drove the fire fighters back; ironwork melted; the roof crashed in; and when dawn came there was nothing left standing. The ferryhouse and depot both were leveled.

The rail-ferry traffic was delayed only briefly, however. That day and the next some trains were routed to other terminals, but soon enough wreckage had been cleared away to give access to most of the slips. Work began at once on plans for a new terminal, and in 1907 it was opened.

There was nothing like it before, and there will never be again—at least not for a ferry. It was immense; railroad officials said the waiting room and concourse could accommodate forty thousand people at one time. It was a splendid structure.

Alighting from their trains, passengers had a choice of routes to the ferries. From the main platform, they could push through swinging doors into the waiting room, cross it and push through other doors into the main ferry shed. To reach the slips of the uptown ferries, they had to make their way through lines of waiting wagons and carriages and dodge those coming off boats just arrived.

However, most of the ferries now had upper decks. To board one of these, passengers could walk from the train platform up a gently sloping broad marble ramp to the concourse on the upper level. This was a tremendous hall, six hundred feet long, majestically high-ceilinged, as ornate as a theater lobby. Along the river side were sliding doors for each slip, each opening onto twin bridges which passengers crossed to go aboard.

The terminal had a fine restaurant, finished in rare woods, bronze, gilt, and gleaming mirrors, with white linen on the tables and attentive waiters. Back in those days there were other niceties, too: the skylights were washed occasionally, and perhaps even the bright work was polished now and then.

But by 1934 the gilt had tarnished, the mirrors dulled, and the grime of a quarter-century lay on every ledge. Since trains and ferries were synchronized, few people ever needed the waiting room; and I often wondered at the vastness of the concourse, for even at rush hour it was barren save for clusters of passengers around each door.

Until the doors slid open, one had no awareness of the river. No windows gave a view of it, nor was there one from the approaching train. The odors were not suggestive of waterfront, either, but compounded of engine stack fumes, coal smoke, and the indescribable bouquet blown from the mouth of the Hudson Tubes, which smell like no other subway on earth.

The Tubes, opened in 1908, offered more or less rapid transit to New York under the river, but in commuting days I would take them only if heavy fog disrupted ferry service. The odor was depressing, but even worse was the screeching of the steel wheels on the short-radius turns, like the sound of finger-nails scraping a blackboard. Anyway, why plunge into a gloomy tunnel when the river was open?

There was a choice of ferries available in the 1930's: to 23rd Street, Christopher Street, or Barclay Street. Mine was Barclay Street. Each morning, when the sliding doors opened, came a moment of anticipation: What was the river like today? What would we see? I hastened across the bridge and around the deck to the far end, for much could be seen even while the ferry was loading.

The river was always choppy, but at times there was a heavy swell, or there might be whitecaps, and in winter we sometimes saw ice-floes. Dutch and Scandinavian liners were at piers just upstream from the ferry. Almost always we saw a liner or two coming up from the Narrows, sometimes a white-hulled cruise ship from the Caribbean, once a file of warships making for anchorage off Riverside Drive. Herring gulls perched on the greenheart piling and wheeled overhead. The background was the skyline of New York, dominated by the Empire State Building.

The whistle blew, bells jangled in the engine-room, the deck vibrated, and we were off. We exchanged whistle signals with an incoming ferry, again with a tug maneuvering toward the Lackawanna freight docks. Then we were clear, the harbor breeze met us, and we turned south, bringing Ellis Island and the Statue of Liberty into view.

By now the passengers had taken up their customary morning routines. On the upper deck, outside, the physical culturists walked two abreast, around and around, twenty circuits between Hoboken and Barclay Street. The more passive nature-lovers sat on the benches outdoors, on the lee side if the wind was raw, but outdoors even in the coldest weather, gloved and muffled. The "deep-water" men took up their stance forward, feet planted solidly, inviting the onslaught of the elements; a few extremists of this category chose positions on the lower deck where they might, on some mornings, taste salt spray.

In the main salon on the upper deck was a coffee bar, which in those days served its brew in real china cups. Here the Rising Young Executives gathered to talk about Big Deals, blocking access to those too timid to shove through them. Meanwhile, Big Deals were actually being made by gray-haired men wearing gray gloves and white scarves, who met by appointment in quiet corners to the rear. The members of Middle Management sat shoulder to shoulder on the rows of benches, as identical as starlings on telephone wires, each behind a copy of the New York *Times* or *Herald-Tribune* folded, New York fashion, vertically down the middle.

The newly hired office boys and clerks roved about uneasily, sometimes clustering in a callow effort to imitate the Rising Young Executives. The dullards were in the cabins below, sitting passively, eyes downcast; some had made the crossing thousands of times without a glance at the river.

Truck-drivers relaxed in their cabs. A handful of early-morning tourists pushed against the rails, staring at the ships, the skyline, and the Statue. Meanwhile Tony—was there ever a shoeshine boy with a name of his own?—made his rounds, pointing accusingly and embarrassingly at every unshined pair of shoes.

The ferries were fast (they could do better than twenty miles per hour) so the crossing was soon made. The captain judged wind and tide, rang for half speed, then for STOP as the ferry dropped into the slip. He crowded against the resilient pilings to lose way, signalled for reverse engines, for STOP again just as she touched, then SLOW AHEAD to hold her while the chains were fastened and the ratchets clanked merrily.

A daily game was played on the upper deck. Two bridges gave access to shore. One deck-hand would open them, each in turn. The challenge to the passengers was to guess which he'd open first, and he had designed any number of strategies to lure the majority to one side while he opened the other.

He was also wise enough to stand aside once the gates were opened, for the front ranks stampeded ashore, some racing to grab taxis, others to beat office time-clocks.

One more pleasure lay ahead for those who had time: we could walk to the subway through Washington Market, where at this very moment the ovens of the Hotloaf Bakery were being opened, and stop for breakfast pastry and coffee. I was, at first, slightly horrified to see other early-morning customers at an adjacent stand eating raw cherrystone clams for breakfast, until I tried it myself one morning and discovered the sweet, briny taste of a really fresh clam, a taste which ice cannot preserve until dinner-time.

Then it was time to board the subway, ride to Grand Central, and walk to my office. Total travel time: one hour and forty minutes, three hours and twenty minutes each working day, sixteen hours and forty minutes each week, eight hundred and thirty-three hours and twenty minutes in a 50-week year.

In the late afternoon, the commuters were subdued going home. They gathered somberly in the Barclay Street ferryhouse, not crowding at the gate, and walked rather than raced aboard when it opened. More of them chose the enclosed lower cabins on this trip, relaxing or sagging on the benches, and no one on the upper deck thought of walking twenty circuits around.

But for me and some fellow-passengers this voyage was a peaceful bridge between work and home. We stood on the upper deck, heads bared to the evening breeze, watching the lights come on, leaving the city to the street-cleaners and charwomen who would prepare it for our return.

By six-thirty the last of the commuters had crossed, save for a few with evening work or theater tickets. Other passengers would cross in the night: late-shift industrial workers, railroad men, and near dawn the drivers of produce trucks. On fair nights there would be others, too, of whom Edna St. Vincent Millay wrote:

> "We were very tired, we were very merry—
> We had gone back and forth all night on the ferry . . ."

For where else could a young couple living in the city's canyons do their courting? Not in the movies or a smoke-layered cafe. Not in crowded Washington Square, or under the eyes of patrolmen in Central Park.

Where else but the ferry, which was right at the end of the street? Two coins in the box, and a moment later the whistle would blow and the city be left behind. Even with no moon or if the sky were overcast, the city's light cast a gentle radiance. At night the upper deck was quiet, and other passengers would keep a little distance away from a couple's chosen spot. For dreamers here was the stuff of a million dreams: the ships, the sky, the gateways to the open ocean, and on the return trip the panorama of the city, land of opportunity, with a million lights in a million windows, each one a star, a career, a hope.

The ferries were the people's yachts, their cruise ships, and the best of all sailed from Whitehall Street, at the lower end of Manhattan, to St. George on Staten Island. This was a half-hour voyage for a nickel. Until a few years ago, the Elevated trains ran all the way from the Bronx to South Ferry, and on hot summer nights, when the windows of the old wooden cars were open, the downtown trains were crowded with couples and families, off for a twenty-cent excursion to cool the hours between supper and bedtime.

On Sundays, too, they came, to stroll around the Battery, visit the old Aquarium with its diving penguins, and sail across the harbor on the ferry. In the past fifty years these Staten Island boats have steamed twenty million miles, with a billion passengers. Ten boats are in service now, and this crossing to St. George is, as yet, untouched by bridge and tunnel builders.

That Staten Island terminal, by the way, obtained its name in an unusual fashion.

When Erastus Wiman achieved domination of the Staten Island Railway he was determined to develop its business. He conceived the idea of a direct ferry route to Manhattan from that point of Staten Island which is closest to the city. There was just one obstacle to be overcome; New York's renowned George Law owned the land upon which Mr. Wiman wanted to put his joint rail-and-ferry terminal.

The railroad magnate approached the landowner and explained his plans. Wiman obtained an option to purchase, but completion of the financial details took longer than at first contemplated. Mr. Wiman was thrice compelled to ask for time extensions. He climaxed his third and very strong appeal with:

"Mister Law, if you will grant me this last extension, I shall not only carry through my project, but I will canonize you!"

George Law was puzzled: "How can you canonize me?"

"Why," exclaimed Wiman, "I will name the new terminal *St. George!*"

And St. George it became and so it has remained, ever since 1886.

But the best is almost the last. Once there were thirteen ferry lines across the East River below 92nd Street; now there are none, save for a short run to Welfare Island, and even that little ferry may soon be gone. At least, it has been scheduled for elimination for quite some time. The Electric Ferries still run across the ship-clustered Narrows between Brooklyn and Staten Island, but on the North River, the Lackawanna has given up all but the Barclay Street line, and a majority of the other railroad ferries are gone.

Night service on the Christopher Street run ended in 1949. Then, on March 31, 1955, Captain William L. Schopf whistled a farewell salute to the ferryhouse on the New York side as the last day trip began, ending 118 years of continuous service. His boat was the 33-year-old *Buffalo*, which began service the year he became Captain. On board for the final trip was a veteran commuter, Mr. A. Schaller of East Orange, New Jersey, who had made the crossing 28,000 times!

Perhaps even these last New York ferries will be gone some day. By the time this book is published only two ferries will remain in San Francisco waters, for the Richmond-San Rafael Bridge will be open then; in 1930 there were 43 in service. The East Boston Municipal Ferry carried passengers for a penny each for 121 years. But this ended in 1953, when the *Charles C. Donaghue* made her last trip. Gone are the ferries of Chicago, Detroit, Baltimore, Philadelphia, and many more cities.

Along the main highways, too, most of the ferries are gone. But America is large, and the adventurous traveler can still find a landscape unmarked by television antennas and billboards. He can still find an unpolluted spring, a night sky undimmed by a city's glow, a stand of virgin timber, and even a ferry.

Not long ago, driving along a dirt road in the Middle West, we came unex-

THE MASTERPIECES OF FRENCH ART, WM. A. ARMSTRONG, ED., 1883

"The Japanese Ferry," painted by Paul Lenoir, 1872. Notice the eyes in the forward part of the boat. The elephant heads suggest that the artist had a substantial imagination. In any event, nothing like *this* ever appeared in America.

pectedly upon a current ferry, a flatboat just big enough for two cars. Within an hour we came upon another.

A few days later we visited Reelfoot Lake, in northwestern Tennessee, a fantastic body of water formed by the great earthquakes of the winter of 1811-12, studded everywhere with the stumps of drowned cypress, surrounded by tall, still-living cypress trees, by beds of lotus, and the vines of wild grape and muscadine. High above were flights of duck and Canada geese. Now like wisps of smoke, once they darkened the skies here.

That afternoon we drove west a mile or two, through the little town of Tiptonville, scene of Commander Walke's gallant dash past Island No. 10, and on to the road's end at the edge of the Mississippi River. The narrow road led through fields, then to the top of the levee, where we stopped to look ahead. Below, the dirt track led to a crude wooden ramp at the water's edge, expendable in any flood. Nearby was a sign, crudely lettered, FERRY. The banks were raw and the marks of old floods were everywhere, debris snagged in trees and bushes. The river, muddy and turbulent, seemed immensely broad and powerful, the far shore little more than a narrow smudge between water and sky.

We could see no boat. I swept the opposite shore with my binoculars, seeing a few low structures but nothing boat-like.

A puff of smoke appeared, the sign of a whistle too distant to hear. Moments later, through the glasses, I could see a tiny shape sliding against the background of the shore. Still later we saw it was making progress toward us; it was the ferryboat.

In this lonesome spot we recaptured the emotion of others who stood here a century ago, for this setting is but little changed. Here was the boundary of one land, old and known and settled. From here one set out on a perilous voyage, on a clumsy chip of a boat, tossed on the mighty Father of Waters. There was no town on the far side, just an obscure landing spot on the muddy bank, and beyond that, the West.

HARPER'S NEW MONTHLY MAGAZINE, AUGUST, 1860